GOSPEL MOTIVATION

More Than "Jesus Died for My Sins"

Robert J.

NORTHWESTERN PUBLISHING HOUSE
Milwaukee, Wisconsin

To the Monday night Bible study group
Good Shepherd's Lutheran Church
West Allis, Wisconsin

Library of Congress Control Number 2006921498
Northwestern Publishing House
1250 N. 113th St., Milwaukee, WI 53226-3284
© 2006 by Northwestern Publishing House
Published 2006
Printed in the United States of America
ISBN 978-0-8100-1977-5

Contents

Foreword

Why Think about Gospel Motivation?

There are several reasons for writing about gospel motivation. First, I have a tremendous need to become more sanctified, more holy, in my life. Perhaps you too have this need. I remember an old teacher saying, "When I was young, I thought that when I was old I would be pious. Now I am old. I am not pious yet." Perhaps all Christians think that way. When we are young, we see the years stretching out before us. "There is time," we say, "time for growth. Things will gradually improve; my strength to resist temptation, to put away pride and ambition, will increase, and I, by God's grace, will have things under control." Sad to say, the years that stretch out before us quickly become the years we see over our shoulders, and reality sets in: "I am not pious yet."

Yes, we do see growth. We do see victories. We do find our understanding and love for God's Word deepen as time gives us the chance to study it and mine its treasures. The wheels of God, which grind slowly but very fine, work on our Christian character, and we see it mature. But often we only see time giving our pet sins and weaknesses the chance to become even more ingrained. What is more, we find ourselves moving into new and uncharted waters where we are just as much novices in Christian living as we were in other areas when we were young. Changes in where we live, the makeup of our families, and our health, and even how life itself changes as we move from one stage to another, present new decisions to make in Christ and new temptations to overcome in him. We know Christ will be with us. Our Christian character matures, and we do not doubt so quickly that Jesus will see us through every change. He will give us help and joy. Nevertheless, we are saddened that we are not yet as pious as we wish to be. Paradoxically, growth in faith and maturity gives us keener insight into our failings and so compounds our problem. But we are confident that the answers to our need for sanctification are all found in Scripture, and this book will aim at finding some of those answers.

The second reason for writing about sanctification stems from how I encouraged my congregations in my sermons to put into practice the instruction I offered them. *Shallow* is a word that comes to mind. Perhaps you remember the old confirmation joke. A veteran confirmation student turns to a new student and says, "Now remember, whatever he asks, just answer, 'Because Jesus died for my sins.' No matter what the question, you'll be okay." It's a joke, but it's not so far from the truth. That may be a parody of confirmation class answers, but it is not so far from the truth in how I encouraged sanctification in my sermons. "The Lord died for you. The Lord loves you. Respond with love and service to God's love for you." There's nothing wrong with that encouragement. But it hardly goes deep enough.

Jesus and the apostles go deeper, much deeper, into the gospel message when they encourage us to serve the Lord. What I am in Christ and how the Lord wants me to live are closely intertwined. I was only using a few strands of thread; the apostles used many strands twisted together into a thick rope that cannot easily be broken. A goal of this book will be to explore the many strands that connect faith and life. The depth and power of God's Word will strengthen in rich and varied ways our ability to speak and encourage others in their lives as God's children.

The third reason to study the link between faith and works as taught in Scripture is to amplify on the basic (and very true) teachings we learned in the catechism. Our Lutheran heritage and the doctrinal statements that are the heart of our heritage are great gifts. At the heart of our heritage is a desire to remain faithful to the gospel. This demands that we use law and gospel carefully. We work hard never to mix the two, that is, turning the law into good news about how I can be right with God or defining the gospel as "good information" on how God wants us to act. To keep these two scriptural teachings separate and to use them as God intended is extremely important for our faith.

So we divide up the teaching. The law shows us our sins. The gospel shows us Christ's redemption. The law shows us how God wants to be served. We work on each part, helping our students and ourselves to keep things straight, for we know that countless errors have been spawned from not keeping these teachings straight.

When we speak about our Christian lives, however, our desire to keep the law and the gospel in a proper relationship often leads us to speak about either one or the other in isolation. In other words, we talk about what Christ has done for us as one topic. Then we talk about some matter of morals as a separate topic. But in our efforts to keep justification and sanctification (faith and life) in their proper places—that is, to properly divide God's Word of Truth—we lose sight of how intimately bound together they are.

The apostles did not divide things like that, even though the division is always apparent in their writings. Their books speak about Christ's work for us, and woven into their gospel is encouragement to live for the Lord. Their books speak about how Christians should live, but all their discussions about life are sprinkled with reminders of what we have become in Christ. The law, the gospel, and our life in Christ are all interwoven. Nothing is omitted. Everything is in perfect balance. Nothing is slighted. These writers could only have been speaking under inspiration of the Holy Spirit, for mere human beings could never speak as perfectly as they did. What a blessing when pastors, in their sermons and Bible studies, imitate the apostles' way of speaking and when all God's people learn to speak that way in conversations with fellow Christians. Hopefully this book will help us arrive at this goal.

The fourth reason for this book is that there is a dark side to the struggle for piety. We have a sinful nature that is quite proficient at taking good pursuits in a wrong direction. A person can want to become pious so fervently, to put away a sin so much, to be so greatly concerned about doing the right thing for the Lord, that he or she begins to search for piety in an impious way.

We will offer a few more thoughts on this point in the final section. But I think it is important to keep this thought in the back of our minds as we think about our own growth in faith. What should be our reasons for growth? Does the gospel really motivate us as we think about what we should do in our lives? Or does the law play a role that it ought not play, leading us to do the right thing for some reason disassociated from the gospel? This book will touch on this theme several times, but for the most part it will be in the background. I think it is enough that we are aware that there is a dark side to piety and then watch how Scripture creates a piety that flows freely from the many-sided gospel.

Hopefully this book will help us develop a healthy view of why we as Christians should strive for piety. This author has no corner on piety. But it is just this lack that has led me to explore the Scripture references in this book. And that is what you will find here—Scripture. This book is not profound in thought. But it is filled with God's Word that, in a simple way, leads us to our goal of life and service in God's kingdom.

Each chapter looks at some aspect of the gospel and shows how it is used in Scripture to encourage us to serve the Lord. In the narrow sense, the gospel is God's work of forgiving the sins of the world and reconciling the world to himself in Christ. Here we widen the term a bit and use it to refer to all the good things God does for us in Christ.

The passages offered here are not the only passages that encourage us to serve the Lord or direct us into some aspect of service. The New Testament is filled with instructions on how to live to please the Lord. Nor are they the only passages that speak about the gospel. There are longer sections that speak about the gospel in more detail (for example, Romans 3–5), where sanctification is not in the writers' minds. We must never lose sight of these passages, for they lay the foundation for the passages we will consider in this book. The gospel passages we have chosen to focus on here are all in close proximity to the writer's encouragement to sanctification. They have been chosen in order to show how the writers weave the gospel into virtually everything they say about our lives in Christ. We will primarily use passages from the New Testament epistles, but we will not limit ourselves to them.

The chapter divisions will help organize the material, but they should not be construed as scriptural divisions. As we go through this study, you may find other aspects of the many-faceted way Scripture links our faith and life. In passages quoted from Scripture, where appropriate, I will highlight the aspect of sanctification the apostle has in mind with *italics* and highlight the gospel motivation in **bold type.** I hope you will sit alongside me at the feet of Jesus and the apostles, and together we will learn something of the art of gospel motivation.

1

The Gospel of God's Love and Forgiveness in Christ

The gospel is big

In this first chapter we will look at the basics. We live our lives for God because he loves us and has forgiven us. Before we look at Scripture, though, we need to understand a few things about gospel motivation itself. To do this, we need to air a little criticism of the sinful nature and some of the paths it leads us down.

In order to identify with and understand the apostles' words about serving the Lord and living our lives for him, we must understand one thing: The gospel is big, very big. It is huge in the minds and hearts of the Bible writers. It is so big that it dominates all their thinking and, therefore, all their actions. Without the gospel and all its blessings in view, they do nothing, they say nothing, and they write nothing.

Let's elaborate on this. Although we speak of gospel motivation, the gospel is never merely a means to that end. It is the end itself. It is God's gift to us. The gospel spurs us to action, but it does so because it is our main focus. It motivates us because it dominates our lives. Unless it does so, it cannot really motivate us.

We are tempted to make the gospel too small in our thinking. We all do this in a number of ways. First, we make the gospel too small when we use it to accomplish our own agendas, as legitimate as those agendas might be. We all have certain needs in our lives. Those needs tend to dominate our thinking. It may be the need for food, for clothing, or for shelter. In our country most of us have enough of these things, so our needs are usually higher up on the hierarchy of needs. We need a sense of fulfillment; we need love from other human beings; we need satisfaction in our jobs. We may need help in our families; we may need help in our marriages; we may need help with parents or in-laws; we may need help with our neighbors. These needs clamor for attention and dominate our views. If those needs become the dominant factor in our lives and if the gospel becomes the means for solving those problems, then the gospel has become too small in our lives.

By nature we tend to focus on the law and how keeping the law affects our lives for the better. The gospel then becomes motivation for keeping the law so that the Lord will bless our lives. When a Christian moves in this direction, the gospel invariably becomes less important and the law becomes more important. This is not to deny that keeping God's law results in blessings for our lives. But if our focus is primarily on these blessings and our means for attaining them become the law— after all, it's something we can do, a method we can understand and follow—the gospel shrinks in importance in our minds; it becomes merely a tool. To put it another way, the gospel becomes extremely important because it is the only thing that can motivate us to keep the law and be blessed. People who think this way seem to value the gospel, but in reality they do not value it as they should.

Not only individual Christians but Christian congregations and church bodies as a whole face this temptation. Congregations rejoice in God's love and forgiveness, and Christians gather to thank and praise God for what he has done. But when a congregation faces difficulties, the gospel tends to shrink and a desire to motivate Christian activity of one sort or another takes its place. For example, when funds are low, sermons on Christian giving are needed, but always with a suitable amount of "gospel motivation." When membership is waning, sermons on reaching out to others are needed, but always with "gospel motivation." When people are being loveless in a congregation, there must be sermons on Christian love, "motivated by the gospel," to be sure.

While you can understand these needs and the desire to motivate fruits of faith by the gospel, the temptation is to shift the emphasis from the gospel to its results and, in the process, to make the gospel too small. Christians in the pews know when the pastor's real agenda is getting them to do something, no matter how clearly he might preach the gospel in the process.

This shift in emphasis results in deadness, not just in our faith in the gospel but in our lives as well. The beautiful and many-faceted way the Bible speaks about our Christian lives becomes pale and lifeless. What results is a monotonous repetition of the basic truths of the gospel. Why? Because the gospel and all it means for us is not our main area of concern and so little time is invested in exploring it and explaining it and seeking scriptural ways to speak about it. It becomes smaller and smaller and less and less a part of our congregation's ministry. It becomes implied in what we do, and what is merely implied is soon lost to our consciousness.

To look at this another way, recall Jesus' statement in the Sermon on the Mount. When he preached against worry, he said, "Seek first his kingdom and his righteousness, and all these things will be given to you as well" (Matthew 6:33). What does the sinful nature do with this passage? It focuses us on "all these things" and suggests that we focus on the gospel and Christ's righteousness so that all these things will be ours. It turns Jesus' words, which he spoke to help us avoid thinking about the things we need in life, into a method to obtain these very things. To the extent that the sinful nature gets us to think this way, the less we put Jesus' words into practice. Jesus is telling us not to worry about these things at all. Focus on the gospel, he tells us. Let that be as big as it deserves to be in your thinking. Let that be your love, your purpose for living, your everything. And when Satan and your sinful nature buck and object that you will lose everything, even what you need for your lives, in the process of focusing on the gospel, then you can comfort yourself with Jesus' words that God will not let you go without. The gospel is never something we use. The gospel is always something that dominates our lives. It is not to be used to effect sanctification. It leads to sanctification. In the fullest sense, holiness of living flows from the gospel only when the gospel is the center of our thinking and more highly valued than the holiness of life that flows from it.

So where is the answer to keeping the gospel big in our minds? One thing is certain: The answer is not found in us. At least I know it is not found in me. By nature I have no love for the gospel or for the One who gave it. All I am concerned about is myself, my needs, my aspirations, my agenda. If there is any love for the gospel in my heart, and by God's grace—amidst all the baggage of self-love—there is, it is there only because of the love God has shown in rescuing me from hell.

The problem of eternal punishment in hell and the goal of eternal life in heaven for everyone on earth is God's agenda. God's purpose in giving us his Word is tied up with this agenda. His agenda is big, bigger than any agenda we might have. All our personal and congregational agendas must revolve around his. There are many ways God has called us to serve him. There are many blessings, even in this life, that come our way as we engage in his work. But all our service and every good thing that comes our way in this life is in some way related to God's ultimate and eternal agenda. This is what we must realize if we are to read with any profit the apostles' words about service to God. I do not come to Scripture asking how Scripture can fix this or that problem. I come to Scripture to learn the problem God wanted to fix and how he has fixed it. I do not use the gospel to help me accomplish my goals, no matter how noble they might be. If my goals line up with God's, then proclaiming the gospel—helping others to know it also—is my goal. Only in this way will we match how the apostles acted and arranged their own lives and how they encouraged others to godly living.

Only God's grace can make our agendas subservient to his. Only God's grace can make us see that his agenda is the only important one. Only his grace can open our eyes to the reality about ourselves, our mortality (and immortality), and his fair and just judgment. Only his grace can lead us to see that our lives are but a speck of time and that eternity is endless; and only his grace can help us shape our agendas around that endless eternity and not the speck of time. Only his grace can lead us to know "how wide and long and high and deep is the love of Christ, and to know this love that surpasses knowledge" (Ephesians 3:18,19).

God's grace can come with the force of God's power as it was displayed to Saul of Tarsus when he saw Jesus and listened to his blinding rebuke (Acts 9:1-6). It can come with the gradual yet profound illumination Luther experienced when he finally realized the meaning of the gospel after years of being in bondage to guilt. Or it can come in the gradual way Timothy must have experienced it, for he had been a believer from infancy and, as far as we know, did not have an earth-shattering experience (2 Timothy 3:14,15). Yet Paul praised him more highly than anyone else, for Timothy's agenda was the same as Paul's.

What can we do so our agenda for gospel motivation imitates Paul's? Nothing except trust that the Lord will enable us to grow in our understanding of his law and gospel so that the gospel and all its blessings will become bigger and bigger in our minds. Scripture is filled with encouragements to grow and promises that God will enable us to do that. Paul's words to the Philippians are particularly appropriate. He writes:

> One thing I do: Forgetting what is behind and straining toward what is ahead, I press on toward the goal to win the prize for which God has called me heavenward in Christ Jesus. All of us who are mature should take such a view of things. And if on some point you think differently, that too

God will make clear to you. Only let us live up to what we
have already attained. (Philippians 3:13-16)

Maturity is straining toward the goal to win the prize—this
is our agenda in life—and for those of us who are not as
mature as Paul, we have his encouragement to live up to what
we have already attained. And where we come up short, we
have Paul's promise that God will make clear to us what was
so clear to Paul.

The gospel is so big that it completely dominated the apostles' thinking. Keep that in mind with every passage you read,
and pray, as I do, that the Lord open our hearts and minds
and that he makes the gospel as big in us as it was in the
apostles. When the gospel fills our thoughts, everything Scripture says about gospel motivation will fall into place.

I've drawn a conclusion without even looking at Scripture.
This is not a legitimate way to start, I know. But this is so
important that I wanted to present it first, perhaps to chal-
lenge you to look at every passage in these chapters to see
whether or not this emphasis is true.

Motivated by the gospel of God's love and
forgiveness in Christ

The gospel, the good news, is that in love God has forgiven
the sins of the world and reconciled the world to himself
through Jesus' work. God has led us to believe the gospel and
to confess that we need it. We will begin with a few basic
passages that encourage us to serve the Lord because of his
love and his forgiveness in Christ. This is where everything
must start.

Notice how the gospel writers remind us in terms of law
and gospel about the great things God has done for us in
Christ. (As a reminder, the bold type highlights the gospel,
and the italic type points to what the gospel leads us to do.)

At one time we too were foolish, disobedient, deceived and
enslaved by all kinds of passions and pleasures. We lived in
malice and envy, being hated and hating one another. **But
when the kindness and love of God our Savior**

appeared, he saved us, not because of righteous things we had done, but because of his mercy. He saved us through the washing of rebirth and renewal by the Holy Spirit, whom he poured out on us generously through Jesus Christ our Savior, so that, having been justified by his grace, we might become heirs having the hope of eternal life. This is a trustworthy saying. *And I want you to stress these things, so that those who have trusted in God may be careful to devote themselves to doing what is good. These things are excellent and profitable for everyone.* (Titus 3:3-8)

Here Paul reminds us that we were delivered from the darkness of sin and the lusts that accompanied it. Notice how Paul talks about the moral depravity we were steeped in. We were foolish and disobedient to God. We were tricked by Satan and bound to live according to his will. Paul then reminds us of our baptism, our rebirth, that we received the Holy Spirit and that God declared us not guilty. Paul reminds us that none of this was our doing but happened only because of God's undeserved kindness and love.

Having reminded Titus of this great gospel blessing, Paul instructs him to stress these truths and to urge those who have come to faith in God to devote their entire lives to doing what is good. Sanctified living is living consistently with the gospel.

Notice how Paul does much the same in Ephesians 2:

As for you, you were dead in your transgressions and sins, in which you used to live when you followed the ways of this world and of the ruler of the kingdom of the air, the spirit who is now at work in those who are disobedient. All of us also lived among them at one time, gratifying the cravings of our sinful nature and following its desires and thoughts. Like the rest, we were by nature objects of wrath. **But because of his great love for us, God, who is rich in mercy, made us alive with Christ even when we were dead in transgressions—it is by grace you have been saved. And God raised us up with Christ and seated us with him in the heavenly realms in Christ Jesus, in order that in the coming ages he might show the incomparable riches of his grace, expressed in his kindness to us in Christ Jesus. For it is by**

grace you have been saved, through faith—and this not from yourselves, it is the gift of God—not by works, so that no one can boast. *For we are God's workmanship, created in Christ Jesus to do good works, which God prepared in advance for us to do.* (Ephesians 2:1-10)

Rejecting God and rejected by him, serving Satan, objects of God's wrath—that's what we were. But we were also objects of God's love and mercy. Paul reminds us that we were saved by grace, through faith, which we did not produce. This gospel, however, produced in us more than eternal salvation. It made us new people. We were created to do good works. Our lives of service to God were in God's will and foreknowledge even before he brought us to faith. When we were brought to faith, we were made people for whom good works are part and parcel of our existence.

The apostle John writes:

How great is the love the Father has lavished on us, that we should be called children of God! And that is what we are! The reason the world does not know us is that it did not know him. **Dear friends, now we are children of God, and what we will be has not yet been made known.** But we know that when he appears, we shall be like him, for we shall see him as he is. *Everyone who has this hope in him purifies himself, just as he is pure.* (1 John 3:1-3)

In these verses John tells us to purify ourselves. Notice the reason why. God loves us and made us his children. Someday we will be changed and glorified. Even now, however, we are pure in God's sight because of Christ's forgiveness. Because of the purity we have in Christ and because of our hope, we will want to purify ourselves in how we live.

In a series of passages, the apostle John weaves together God's love for us and our love for him and our fellowman:

This is how God showed his love among us: He sent his one and only Son into the world that we might live through him. **This is love: not that we loved God, but that he loved us and sent his Son as an atoning sacrifice for our sins.** Dear friends, **since God so loved us,** *we also* *ought to love one another. We love* **because he first loved us.** (1 John 4:9-11,19)

This is how we know what love is: **Jesus Christ laid down his life for us.** *And we ought to lay down our lives for our brothers.* (1 John 3:16)

Note the link. Love begins with God's love in sending his Son to atone for our sins. His love gives rise to our love and is the reason we strive to serve him.

Read over the following passages, and find the link between God's love and God's will for us to live lives of service.

The life I live in the body, I live by faith in the Son of God, who loved me and gave himself for me. (Galatians 2:20)

As a prisoner for the Lord, then, I urge you to live a life worthy of the calling you have received. (Ephesians 4:1)

Bear with each other and forgive whatever grievances you may have against one another. Forgive as the Lord forgave you. (Colossians 3:13)

Be kind and compassionate to one another, forgiving each other, just as in Christ God forgave you. Be imitators of God, therefore, as dearly loved children and live a life of love, just as Christ loved us and gave himself up for us as a fragrant offering and sacrifice to God. (Ephesians 4:32–5:2)

In the next passage, Peter encourages his readers to grow in the virtues fostered by the Spirit. Notice the last sentence. Lack of virtue results if a person doesn't remember and appreciate the fact that he has been cleansed from his sins.

For this very reason, make every effort to add to your faith goodness; and to goodness, knowledge; and to knowledge, self-control; and to self-control, perseverance; and to perseverance, godliness; and to godliness, brotherly kindness; and to brotherly kindness, love. *For if you possess these qualities in increasing measure, they will keep you from being ineffective and unproductive in your knowledge of our Lord Jesus Christ.* But if anyone does not have them, he is nearsighted and blind, and has forgotten that he has been **cleansed from his past sins.** (2 Peter 1:5-9)

In the next passage, Paul issues a strong warning. If we willingly keep on sinning, we will forfeit our place in God's kingdom. But his warning is not a cold command. Paul reminds his readers and us that we were made members of God's kingdom through his love and forgiveness. We were washed, sanctified, and justified. That wonderful status is what we want to hold on to.

> Do you not know that the wicked will not inherit the kingdom of God? Do not be deceived: Neither the sexually immoral nor idolaters nor adulterers nor male prostitutes nor homosexual offenders nor thieves nor the greedy nor drunkards nor slanderers nor swindlers will inherit the kingdom of God. *And that is what some of you were.* **But you were washed, you were sanctified, you were justified in the name of the Lord Jesus Christ and by the Spirit of our God.** (1 Corinthians 6:9-11)

Note the beautiful picture Paul paints in the following passage:

> Your boasting is not good. Don't you know that a little yeast works through the whole batch of dough? *Get rid of the old yeast that you may be a new batch without yeast—* **as you really are. For Christ, our Passover lamb, has been sacrificed.** *Therefore let us keep the Festival, not with the old yeast, the yeast of malice and wickedness, but with bread without yeast, the bread of sincerity and truth.* (1 Corinthians 5:6-8)

We are like the Passover bread, cleansed through Christ's sacrifice. For this reason we are to keep the Passover festival by putting off malice and wickedness and using the bread of sincerity and truth.

Finally, Paul reminds us of God's grace and salvation. Christ redeemed us, that is, he bought us back to be God's possession, and as God's possession we are to put off wickedness and purify ourselves, for we are a people who "are his very own."

> **The grace of God that brings salvation has appeared to all men.** *It teaches us to say "No" to ungodliness and worldly passions, and to live self-controlled, upright and*

godly lives in this present age, **while we wait for the blessed hope—the glorious appearing of our great God and Savior, Jesus Christ, who gave himself for us to redeem us from all wickedness and to purify for himself a people that are his very own,** *eager to do what is good.* These, then, are the things you should teach. Encourage and rebuke with all authority. Do not let anyone despise you. (Titus 2:11-15)

Did you see how the writers drew us outside ourselves and into the hope of the gospel, something much bigger than our existence here and now? Did you see how they based their encouragement to us on the tremendous blessings we have in Christ? Did you see how big the gospel was in their minds and how it dominated everything they said? We will see this again and again as we expand on the many facets of God's good news in Christ.

2

The Gospel of Death and Life

Romans 6:1-13

The New Testament writers saw the gospel as the heart and center of their existence. Everything they said and did was shaped around the gospel, for the gospel was their greatest treasure, rising above anything this world offered. Through their letters, the apostles worked to encourage Christians to hold fast to the gospel and live to serve the Lord who loves them and forgave their sins.

In their zeal, the apostles looked at the gospel from many standpoints and brought each one to bear on the lives of God's people. That is the purpose of this book, to explore the many ways they did this.

A good place to start is with the gospel of death and life. It is where Paul led the Romans in chapter 6 of his letter to the Romans. This chapter and the first half of chapter 7 occupy a strategic place in the book of Romans. In the first five chapters, Paul reviewed the law and the gospel. He reminded the Romans about God's wrath that was being poured out on the world because the world chose to worship idols rather than God. But then he reminded them about the mercy and grace God poured out on the world through his Son, Jesus, who died for all sins and calls people to repent and believe and be saved from God's wrath.

After Paul reviewed the gospel message in Romans, he did something unique in his writings. He did not immediately talk about special ways his readers should serve the Lord. He did not deal with personal sin, congregational problems, or special instructions the Romans needed. Rather, he explained (but hardly in an academic way) their new relationships with Christ, sin, and the law. He would talk about specific ways the Romans should serve the Lord beginning in chapter 12. But here in chapters 6 and 7, Paul talks about the foundation of gospel motivation. In fact, chapter 6 begins a complete discussion, going on for three chapters, of how Christians should view their new lives in Christ.

In the first half of chapter 6 and the first six verses of chapter 7, Paul talks about the gospel in terms of death and life. Christians are to view themselves as both dead and alive. He asks us:

> What shall we say, then? Shall we go on sinning so that grace may increase? By no means! **We died to sin;** *how can we live in it any longer?* (6:1,2)

Paul's critics seem to have accused him of encouraging people to sin more so that God could forgive them more. (Actually, Paul is encouraging people to look at the law and uncover just how much they have sinned, confess their sins to God, and receive forgiveness.) Paul defends himself against that idea. He is saying, "We are the kind of people who have died to sin. How can we go on living a life of sin?"

Now Paul brings in the gospel of death and life, if we can be permitted to call it that. He writes:

> Don't you know that all of us who were baptized into Christ Jesus were baptized into his death? **We were therefore buried with him through baptism into death in order that, just as Christ was raised from the dead through the glory of the Father,** *we too may live a new life.* (6:3,4)

Baptism does great things. Through our baptism, we were joined with Jesus in his death and we were buried with him into his death. We died so that we might rise to life again. The NIV translation "we too may live a new life" sounds like this in the Greek: "in order that we too might walk in the newness of life." The term Paul uses here for "walk" he usually uses in reference to what we do in life, that is, the things we do to serve God. "Newness of life" is a new kind of existence, a new status before God, which is the context for our new "walk."

Paul continues to explain the change that has come about in us.

> If we have been united with him like this in his death, we will certainly also be united with him in his resurrection. (6:5)

We must be careful here. At first glace it sounds as if Paul is talking about the resurrection of our bodies on the Last Day. But from the context (note verse 11) we see that he is talking about a resurrection we are enjoying right now, the "newness of life" he just referred to. Paul uses the word *will* as we do when we say, "If it's light out, the sun will be shining." The idea is more logical than future—in other words, "If *this* happens, then *that* will necessarily happen also." If we were joined with Jesus in death at our baptism, then it is logical that we will also be joined with him in his resurrection—and we are. Paul literally says that we are joined with Jesus in the "likeness of his death" and in the "likeness of his resurrection," telling us that he is not necessarily talking about our physical death and resurrection.

The next verses spell out what happened to Jesus and also what happened to us since we were joined to him.

> We know that our old self was crucified with him so that the body of sin might be done away with, that we should no longer be slaves to sin—because anyone who has died has been freed from sin. Now if we died with Christ, we believe that we will also live with him. (6:6-8)

Simply put, if we have died, we have been freed from sin. A person who has died is no longer under the law, nor is that person subject to the compulsions of the sinful nature. Paul continues:

> We know that since Christ was raised from the dead, he cannot die again; death no longer has mastery over him. The death he died, he died to sin once for all; but the life he lives, he lives to God. In the same way, count yourselves dead to sin but alive to God in Christ Jesus. (6:9-11)

The work of Christ is complete. He conquered sin completely, and his victory makes it so that he will never have to die again. He died once, and when he died, he died for all. Now he lives to serve God the Father, sitting at his right hand, ruling over all things for the good of the church and ushering in the Last Day, when he will complete his work by judging the world and creating a new heaven and a new earth.

This sense of finality—Jesus' final victory over death and a life of ongoing service to his heavenly Father is now transferred to us. Paul tells us to "count" ourselves, that is, to evaluate our situation as children of God and realize that the same is true for us. We died with Christ, and so we are dead to sin. We were raised to life with Christ, and now we live to serve God.

This is very good news. At the Last Supper, Jesus said to his disciples, "I am the vine; you are the branches. If a man remains in me and I in him, he will bear much fruit; apart from me you can do nothing" (John 15:5). But what does it mean to remain in Jesus? To believe in him and to believe that he loves us and is our Savior? Certainly! But notice in Romans 6 how Paul expands on that basic gospel. We remain in Christ when we think about the fact that we joined him in his death and resurrection. We remain in him when we consider the result of dying with him—our old nature died and we were taken out of the realm where sin can touch us. And we remain in him when we realize that we are joined in his resurrection—enjoying a new life free from sin in which we can serve the Lord.

Based on this gospel of death and life, Paul encourages us to serve the Lord. But the gospel does not simply motivate us to do something. It is also the message about an entirely new state of being that we enjoy in Christ. Because this is so—because the gospel has made such a radical change in our status before God, indeed, in our very existence in this life—this is what we are to do:

> *Do not let sin reign in your mortal body so that you obey its evil desires. Do not offer the parts of your body to sin, as instruments of wickedness, but rather offer yourselves to God,* **as those who have been brought from death to life;** *and offer the parts of your body to him as instruments of righteousness.* (6:12,13)

Here Paul gives us general directions on what to do. The specifics will come later. Notice how our death and life in Christ are the foundation of our lives of faith. That is what we *are:* people who have been brought from death to life. He doesn't want us to forget it, as we are so prone to do. We are to serve the Lord for this reason—not for any personal advantage we might gain from doing so, but because we have died with Christ and are now alive with him.

The final verse of this section hints at where Paul is going in the last part of chapter 6 and the first part of chapter 7. Paul writes, "Sin shall not be your master, because you are not under law, but under grace" (6:14). This verse leads us into the topic of the next chapter, so we'll wait until then to talk about it.

Other places in Scripture

Let's turn our attention to other places in Scripture that talk about the gospel of death and life and its implications for our lives. Paul used this thought in his letter to the Galatians. He wrote:

> *Through the law I died to the law so that I might live for God.* **I have been crucified with Christ and I no longer live, but Christ lives in me.** *The life I live in the body,* **I live by faith in the Son of God, who loved me and gave himself for me.** (Galatians 2:19,20)

Through the law, that is, when the law convicted Paul of his sins so that he realized his need for a Savior and came to faith in Christ, he died to the law. That is, when Paul came to faith in Christ, he died along with Christ and entered a new existence where he had nothing to do with the law. After Paul died with Christ, he rose with him and now has an existence in which living a life for God is a reality.

In Romans 6 Paul talked about being buried with Christ into his death. Here in Galatians, Paul links himself intimately with the way Jesus died—crucifixion. Paul came to see that when Jesus died on the cross, he, Paul, was there also. He also speaks of life in rich terms that bind him intimately with Christ. The new life he lives for God, he lives because Christ lives in him. Paul is reflecting what Jesus told his disciples when he told them, "If a man remains in me *and I in him,* he will bear much fruit; apart from me you can do nothing" (John 15:5). So to die with Christ and to live with him means that we see ourselves crucified with him and know that he has come to live in us. All this is Christ's doing, our death and our life.

See how Paul further speaks about the good news of our death in Christ:

> Those who belong to Christ Jesus have crucified the sinful nature with its passions and desires. (Galatians 5:24)

The sinful nature in us has died through our participation in the death of Christ, and when the old nature died, its passions and desires died too.

Paul once more refers to this concept—this reality that all Christians take part in. He writes:

> May I never boast except in the cross of our Lord Jesus Christ, through which the world has been crucified to me, and I to the world. (Galatians 6:14)

All the demands of God's law, which only result in futile efforts to serve God because the sinful nature is powerless, all the pride that naturally comes from the fleeting and empty "successes" we have under the law, all of this is swallowed up in one truth: we died with Christ and now enjoy a new existence totally unlike anything this law-driven world can offer. And this is the new existence you and I share.

The gospel of death—I feel rather foolish calling it that, but it is really true—comes up again in the book of Colossians. One of the reasons Paul wrote the book of Colossians was to correct false ideas about Christ. In that letter Paul shows Christ for all he is. In the process Paul brings our lives into the mix. In one place Paul says that "in Christ all the fullness of the Deity lives in bodily form" (2:9). He tells us the good news that we have been given fullness in Christ. We have been given a new way of existing in which we serve God as he wants to be served.

Paul tells us that we were circumcised by Christ. (Circumcision was a Jewish custom that symbolized putting off the sinful nature. The concept, not the act, applied to men and women alike.) How? Paul explains:

> . . . with the circumcision done by Christ, having been buried with him in baptism and raised with him through your faith in the power of God, who raised him from the dead. (Colossians 2:11,12)

On Easter we confess Christ's resurrection by the power of God. We also confess our own resurrection in him. Our entire existence has been changed. No longer do we serve merely by following the rules. Paul rebuked the Colossians and rebukes us for falling back into that way of thinking. He writes:

> **Since you died with Christ to the basic principles of this world,** *why,* as though you still belonged to it, *do you submit to its rules:* "Do not handle! Do not taste! Do not touch!"? (Colossians 2:20,21)

Then he stresses what we have become, adding some new facets to the gospel of death and life:

> **Since, then, you have been raised with Christ,** *set your hearts on things above,* where Christ is seated at the right hand of God. *Set your minds on things above, not on earthly things.* **For you died, and your life is now hidden with Christ in God. When Christ, who is your life, appears, then you also will appear with him in glory.** (Colossians 3:1-4)

Our death and resurrection with Christ also means that we have ascended with Christ into heaven, not physically but spiritually. It means that right now you are in heaven, hidden with Christ in God. We often think of the Last Day, when we will see Jesus come again with glory. And those believers who are alive in Christ will, in fact, see him when he comes—we might be there too! But in a spiritual way, as Paul says, we will actually come *with* Christ when he appears, and because we have died and risen with him, we will appear *with* him in the same glory of holiness and perfection that he has.

This is big! This is more than a tool for motivation. This is a reality that extends beyond this world. And our response to it should be in line with its magnitude:

> Put to death, therefore, whatever belongs to your earthly nature: sexual immorality, impurity, lust, evil desires and greed, which is idolatry. (Colossians 3:5)

In the next passages we're going to look at, Paul uses this truth to encourage Timothy. He quotes what must have been a hymn sung by the church of his day. The hymn was written to encourage Christians to hold on to their faith and not to renounce it in the face of resentment and persecution from the world. It is interesting that the fact of our death in Christ and all that means was the truth the church employed to help it resist the trials it faced—to motivate itself to stand firm:

> Here is a trustworthy saying:
> If we died with him,
>   we will also live with him;
> if we endure,
>   we will also reign with him.
> If we disown him,
>   he will also disown us;

if we are faithless,
>   he will remain faithful, for he cannot disown himself.
(2 Timothy 2:11-13)

A couple more passages will round out our discussion of the gospel of death and life. This message motivated Paul to do mission work. Here Paul's use of the idea of death is a little different from his use of it in the passages above. Here the gospel of death is Christ's own death, yet it motivates Paul to action. Paul wrote to the Corinthians:

> Christ's love compels us, because we are convinced that **one died for all, and therefore all died. And he died for all,** *that those who live should no longer live for themselves but for him* **who died for them and was raised again.**
> (2 Corinthians 5:14,15)

The context of this passage is Paul's evangelism work. He said that he was compelled by the love of Christ for all people. When Paul looked at the world, what did he see? Amazingly, he saw people who had died in Christ. Here he is not talking about Christians who have died and come to life through repentance and faith. Rather, he is talking about what has happened to the whole world. Remember what Jesus said in John 12:31,32:

> Now is the time for judgment on this world; now the prince of this world will be driven out. But I, when I am lifted up from the earth, will draw all men to myself.

"Men" in this verse, of course, means "people." Jesus said that when he was lifted up from the earth on the cross, he would draw all people to himself. In his person the Son of Man gathered all of us into himself. At that point he joined all people with himself in death, in anticipation of the day they would believe this truth, come to life by faith, and live for him.

Paul's work was to preach this truth so that people would believe it and accept what happened to them in Christ when he died. He wanted this message to lead as many as possible to believe the gospel of their death in Christ so that they might rise again and live not for themselves but for the One who shared his death and resurrection with them.

What a powerful motivation for our mission work! Everyone we see has already died with Christ, which proves that he loves every one of them and has saved them from their sins. Their only need is to know it and believe it.

I must admit that I haven't preached the gospel of death and life as I should have. But when you consider that here in Romans 6 is where Paul started his discussion on why we should serve the Lord, you realize what an important part of the gospel and of gospel motivation this truth is.

An old African-American spiritual included in our hymnal asks some questions: "Were you there when they crucified my Lord? Were you there when they nailed him to the tree? Were you there when they laid him in the tomb?" (*Christian Worship* [CW] 119). Every Christian can say, "Yes, I was there when they crucified my Lord, for he took me into himself when he went to the cross. Yes, I was there when they nailed him to the tree, for I was nailed there with him. Yes, I was there when they laid him in the tomb, for at my baptism I was buried with him into death." But go on! "I was there when he rose and came out of the tomb, and I share his resurrection life. And I was there when he ascended into heaven, and I am there with him right now, and my real life is kept secure in the almighty God."

Sometimes it causes me to tremble. But more often it causes me to think. This aspect of the gospel is heady stuff. Mel Gibson's movie *The Passion of the Christ* was a powerful portrayal of all that Jesus suffered for our sins. It may have had some faults, but its message moved hearts to tears. I find Paul's message about my death and life with Christ to be rather intellectual, but no less spiritual. I personally have not plumbed the depths of what it means to die with Christ and live with him. It is something that will take more study and meditation. But even an imperfect understanding provides the foundational reason for what I do in my life. It is also closely linked with other aspects of the gospel that we will explore in the next two chapters.

3

The Gospel of Slavery
to Righteousness

Romans 6:14-23

There are times in a Christian's life when it appears that he or she may be sitting on the fence, serving both the Lord and the sinful flesh. In fact, at times every Christian appears to be doing that. At these times we become confused. Maybe we doubt our Christianity. Maybe we doubt God, thinking he has let us drift in our sins. Maybe we consider giving up. After all, Jesus said, "No one can serve two masters. Either he will hate the one and love the other, or he will be devoted to the one and despise the other. You cannot serve both God and Money" (Matthew 6:24). We wonder which master is really riding us.

Paul concludes the first section of Romans 6 with these words: "Sin shall not be your master, because you are not under law, but under grace" (verse 14). At hearing this, the sinful nature perks up its ears. The sinful nature is looking for every excuse it can to find sin. Paul's talk about not being under the law and living in the light of God's grace and forgiveness seems to provide such an excuse. If we do not live under the law and are given God's grace, then we have free reign to sin, right? Wrong. It's just the opposite. Paul explains why, and in the process he gives us one of the most powerful reasons why we serve the Lord.

The point of Romans 6:14-23 is simple. By God's grace we have become slaves to righteousness. Paul starts out by saying:

> Don't you know that when you offer yourselves to someone to obey him as slaves, you are slaves to the one whom you obey—whether you are slaves to sin, which leads to death, or to obedience, which leads to righteousness? (6:16)

Two options. That's all there is. It may seem that we can sit on the fence, but we really can't. Slavery is a fact of life. There is no such thing as freedom from a master who controls your thoughts and actions. Before Christ there was only one master, one thing that rode our hearts, and that was sin. And when the rider Sin controlled the reins of our lives, we found ourselves plummeting into the abyss of eternal death.

But when we were brought to faith, we found out that another rider wants to ride us—and he does ride us. This is Jesus Christ. There is something else to which we can be slaves: "to obedience, which leads to righteousness." This is perhaps the hardest phrase in this section to understand. It doesn't really form a parallel with the first phrase, "slaves to sin, which leads to death." Our first reaction is to make the two phrases parallel. "Sin" in the first phrase is interpreted as sinning, and "obedience" in the second phrase is interpreted as doing the right thing. Sinning leads to death; doing the right thing leads to righteousness. This interpretation is not necessarily wrong. Yet we might consider another interpretation. We will do this in the next several paragraphs and then offer a summary. These are perhaps the most technical paragraphs in the book. Yet understanding the two phrases "sin, which leads to death" and "obedience, which leads to righteousness" are crucial to understanding the gospel of slavery to righteousness.

In verses 16 through 18, the key words are "obedience" *(obey)*, and "righteousness." Verse 17 helps us understand the meaning of "obedience." In verse 17 Paul is clearly speaking about something his readers did in the past. They "wholeheartedly obeyed the form of teaching to which [they] were entrusted." In the word *obey,* Paul is clearly referring to faith. Using the word *obey* in this way may sound strange to us, but it is perfectly normal for Paul. To come to faith is the "obedience" of faith. It is to obey God when he tells us to give up our own righteousness and submit ourselves to finding our hope in the righteousness Christ has won for us. In Romans 10:3,4, Paul explains the tragic mistake of the Jewish people in general: "Since they did not know the righteousness that comes from God and sought to establish their own, they did not submit to God's righteousness. Christ is the end of the law so that there may be righteousness for everyone who believes." Faith, therefore, can be spoken of as an act of obedience in which God, through his Holy Spirit, enables us to see our complete unworthiness to stand before him and humbly submit to his way of finding access to him.

Getting back to Romans 6, we understand "obedience" in verse 17 to be faith. It is obedience to the "form of teaching," which is the gospel message; it is obedience "to which you were entrusted" by God's grace. This obedience leads to righteousness, Christ's righteousness, and it makes us "slaves to righteousness" (verse 18).

Martin Franzmann, in his commentary on Romans, writes concerning verse 16:

> The alternative to [the slavery to sin] is a slavery too. Paul calls it, rather strangely, a slavery to obedience. This "obedience" is the religious act which Paul has previously called "the obedience of faith" and of which he will speak again in the next verse. It is the basic surrender of man's liberated will to the call and claim of God, the source of all concrete acts of obedience to His will; it "leads to righteousness" and

> therefore to life (cf. 1:17; 6:23) *(Romans: A Commentary,*
> St. Louis: Concordia, 1968, p. 117.)

That Paul is talking about the obedience of faith, which gives us a new status before God in Christ, becomes clear in verse 22. There Paul speaks about our being slaves to righteousness as being "slaves to God," who has called us to faith. This is the contrast Paul wants to make. Either we are slaves to sin (which we commit) or slaves to righteousness (which we have as a gift).

At this point the emphasis is on the thing to which we are slaves, not so much the actions we do as slaves. We can say, "I'm a slave to Mr. Smith." Or we can say, "I'm a slave to picking cotton." The two refer to the same thing, but the first stresses the one who dictates my actions, and the other stresses what the master wants me to do. In Romans 6:15 and following, Paul is stressing the one who owns me. These two phrases we have been looking at in verse 16 can be summarized as follows: My owner is either the principle of sin in my sinful flesh, which always reacts to God's law by doing the opposite of what God wants. Or it is a life filled with the righteousness of Christ, which frees me from the law and drives me forward into a life of righteousness.

In verses 14-23, then, Paul is talking about the status we have before God. Either we live our lives in the same status we had when we were born, namely, in slavery to sin, or we live in the new status that God has given us, in slavery to Christ's righteousness, which God has given us as a gift. So Paul is proceeding in the same way he did in the first section of chapter 6. He talked there about a status we have with God. In verses 1-14 it was being joined with Christ's death through Baptism and rising with him into a new life free from sin. Here it is a change of masters, in which God freed us from the slave-master of sin and taught us to believe in Christ, to be filled with his righteousness and to be slaves to that righteousness. What Baptism did for us is paralleled by what the Word does for us. Baptism and the Word are both channels of God's grace; God is the agent, and we are the recipients. Through Baptism and faith in the Word of forgiveness, we have received a new status whose liberating power provides both the reason and the motive for serving God. In both cases Paul is unfolding for us the simple gospel message and showing in concrete terms the implications of faith in this gospel.

In the first half of Romans 6, Paul urged sanctified living like this: "Therefore do not let sin reign in your mortal body" (verse 12). In the second half of Romans 6, Paul encourages us like this:

> Just as you used to offer the parts of your body in slavery to impurity and to ever-increasing wickedness, *so now offer them in slavery to righteousness leading to holiness.* When you were slaves to sin, you were free from the control of righteousness. What benefit did you reap at that time from the things you are now ashamed of? Those things result in death! **But now that you have been set free from sin and have become slaves to God,** the benefit you reap leads to holiness, and the result is eternal life. (6:19-22)

This is nothing other than what Jesus said in Matthew 6:24: "No one can serve two masters. Either he will hate the one and love the other, or he will be devoted to the one and despise the other." Slavery to sin leads to ever-increasing wickedness and, finally, to death. Slavery to righteousness leads to holiness of life, and the end of this kind of life on earth is eternal life in heaven. This is true gospel motivation. What power lies in these words!

Paul concludes this section with a beautiful verse, one many Christians memorize: "The wages of sin is death, but the gift of God is eternal life in Christ Jesus our Lord" (6:23). Slavery to righteousness—slavery to God—does not earn anything for us. In the previous verse, the NIV translates, "The benefit you reap leads to holiness, and the result is eternal life." The word *result* may give a person the wrong impression. A result is the outcome of what I do. What I do has a bearing on the result. The NIV translation may lead someone to think that what he or she does in slavery to God causes the result, eternal life, to happen. The Greek word is much more neutral. It is most often translated "end." In other words, the "end" of life lived in slavery to God is eternal life.

Paul clears up any misunderstanding in the last verse of the chapter. Slavery to sin will earn its wages: eternal death. It does indeed cause its result. But slavery to righteousness and to God is a gift of God. He entrusted to us the message of the gospel; he gave us righteousness and made us slaves to it; he established the "end" of our lives as his slaves—eternal life. We all must admit that we are unworthy slaves (Luke 17:10; NIV translates as "servants") and acknowledge that the "end" of our slavery, eternal life, is a gift of God.

Paul uses this concept of slavery later in Romans 7:25. We will look at that in another chapter. Unlike his discussion of dying and living with Christ and his next discussion about the freedom of the Spirit (7:1-6), Paul does not use the picture of slavery elsewhere in his letters. In 6:19 he told the Romans, "I put this in human terms because you are weak in your natural selves." Perhaps Paul's use of "human terms" was suitable for what he wanted to tell the Romans, but it did not fit well into other contexts.

Nevertheless, the concept of Christian slavery to God is found throughout Scripture (see Hebrews 2:14,15 and 2 Peter 2:19), and all discussions of sanctification imply that how we live is not ours to decide. Paul called himself a slave of Christ in Romans 1:1, Philippians 1:1, and Titus 1:1. The NIV translates the Greek word as "servant." Perhaps the translators wanted to avoid the negative connotation of the word *slave*. Whatever their reasons, the translation "servant" in these passages doesn't do justice to Paul's thought. A servant is someone who can choose whom he wants to work for. He can come and go for the day; he has time off and can enjoy vacations. He gets paid for his work. A slave, on the other hand, is bound to one person, without pay, every minute of his life. He cannot choose a different master. That's how Paul saw himself in relation to God. He was not a servant; he was a slave.

That's what we are too. And what a wonderful slavery it is! Imagine you had a stockbroker who was always right in his investment advice. He was so good that he gained 50 percent a year on your investments. Whatever stock he told you to invest in was always a winner. What's more, this broker promised that he would never go off looking for a client with deeper pockets and leave you to your own decisions. He would stay with you forever. All you had to do was shape all your thinking and strategies around him and his advice. In effect, he wanted you to become his slave. Would you buck at that kind of slavery? Would you resent being a slave to that kind of person? I wouldn't.

That's what it's like being a slave to God. He has given you his righteousness, which lays the foundation for a life of peace now and a life in his presence in eternity. He promises that all things will work out for your good as you walk the road to eternal life. He daily blesses you with good things. You are completely protected from the power of sin as long as you live under his care. Who will buck at that kind of slavery? Who will resent giving their lives as slaves to that kind of person? This is slavery stripped of all negative connotations. This is slavery a person can be proud of. There should be lines of people waiting to become slaves of such a master.

Thoughts on head and heart knowledge

There is an issue we must face when it comes to gospel motivation. Pastors and teachers especially should be concerned about this, but all Christians should be concerned about it too. It's one of those issues—actually it is a way of talking—that is naturally cleared up when a person understands gospel motivation. The statement comes in two forms. First, the statement is made that if we are going to have an effect on people's lives, we have to speak not just to their heads but to their hearts as well. Or, Christianity is not just head knowledge; it is heart knowledge. Second, the statement is made that if Christian teachers are going to have an influence, they must teach people not just so their heads are filled with knowledge but so they are moved to action.

But how do we speak to the head and to the heart? How do we teach so that we effect a change in a person? I have to admit that the whole distinction between head and heart knowledge puzzles me. Or to use another term that is used to describe good teaching today, I am really not sure how I should be teaching "affectively."

How did Paul teach? Remember, the section at which we have been looking (Romans 6) is at the heart of his teaching about the Christian life. If there is any place he should be teaching to the heart, and if there is any place he should be teaching "affectively," it is here. So how does he do it? He appeals to what we know. He amplifies on the gospel that all of us hold dear. Notice how many times he appeals to what we know (for Western audiences, what we have stored in our head): "Don't you know" (verse 3); "for we know" (verse 6); "we believe" (verse 8); "for we know" (verse 9); "count yourselves" (verse 11); "don't you know" (verse 16); "you wholeheartedly obeyed the form of teaching" (verse 17). Paul appeals to what his readers know, and he expands on their knowledge; he explains what the gospel means and describes in vivid terms the status we have as people who obey the gospel.

If we are to learn anything from Paul's method of encouraging sanctification, it is this: Explain the gospel and expand on the gospel. Describe in as many ways as you can what the gospel means for that Christian friend who needs to be built up in the faith. "What does the gospel mean for you? This is what it means. . . ." "What have you become as one who believes the gospel? This is what you have become. . . ." "How should you live as a child of God? This is how you should live, and as I explain this to you, I will also tell you why you should live this way."

If there is just criticism that Christian teachers appeal too much to the head and not enough to the heart, it has nothing to do with their manner of speaking, their sincerity, their body language, or any of that. It may be that too much Bible study time is wasted on biblical facts or on a close examination of the laws of God. Too much time is spent on side matters in order to avoid wrestling with the gospel and, through it, seeing the depth of God's love for us. (This is a strong statement, I know. But forgive me, dear reader, for I am speaking to myself if not to you.) If we mine the depth of Scripture and ask the Lord to teach us through those words to better know our inheritance in Christ, we will never be speaking merely to the head but always to the heart as well.

The sad thing about speaking of head versus heart when we talk about motivating Christians to action is that the head always comes up short. Yet knowledge, cognitive perception, of the gospel is what we need above all else, and shortchanging the mind may be setting up a roadblock to the very thing that alone will lead us to grow to live as God's willing slaves. Scripture does indeed make a distinction between heart and mind. Jesus said, "Love the Lord your God with all your *heart* and with all your soul and with all your *mind* and with all your strength" (Mark 12:30). Yet analyze this verse from Paul:

> I pray also that the *eyes* of your *heart* may be *enlightened* in order that you may *know* the hope to which he has called you, the riches of his glorious inheritance in the saints. (Ephesians 1:18)

It is hard to separate head and heart in that passage. To know the hope to which the Lord has called us is to have hearts filled with a desire to please the Lord. Or consider this passage:

> I pray that out of his glorious riches he may strengthen you with power through his Spirit in your inner being, so that Christ may dwell *in your hearts through faith.* And I pray that you, being rooted and established in love, may have power, together with all the saints, *to grasp* how wide and long and high and deep is the love of Christ, *and to know* this love that surpasses knowledge—that you may be filled to the measure of all the fullness of God. (Ephesians 3:16)

That pretty much says it all. We are doing our work as Christian teachers if we lead people into the depth of the gospel and then pray that God use our words to strengthen our hearers, praying that the Lord will establish them in his love so that they can understand that love to its furthest limit. Then we will reach the heart, mind, emotions, will, personality, and whatever other categories we may assign to the spiritual side of our beings.

To encourage teachers to speak to the head and heart may have its place. But it seems more constructive simply to examine sections of Scripture like Romans 6 and pattern our preaching and teaching on Paul's way of speaking. Doing that, we will cover all the bases.

4

The Gospel of True Spirituality

Romans 7:1-6

In Galatians 5:16 Paul writes, "Live by the Spirit, and you will not gratify the desires of the sinful nature." This is a very powerful and far-reaching statement. It offers complete victory over the sinful nature. The only thing we need to know is what it means to "live by the Spirit."

The title of this chapter is a little outside Scripture's normal way of speaking. The term *true spirituality* is more in tune with book titles found on the shelves of Christian bookstores. Yet *true spirituality,* if we agree to use that term, leads us into a discussion we must have if we are to truly appreciate how Scripture defines that term.

So what is spirituality? *Spiritual* is one of the most commonly used words in secular conversations about religion. What does it mean to you if I say, "That person is deeply spiritual"?

If you were Roman Catholic, you might think of monks and nuns as very spiritual people. You might think of their strict adherence to the rules of their monasteries and convents, their intense and regulated prayer life, the vows they take, the meditation they engage in. These people seek to put down the body and mind in order to cultivate the spirit, in contrast to the average person's search for bodily pleasures.

If you were a member of the charismatic or Pentecostal communities, your definition of *spiritual* might tend in the direction of miraculous gifts or perhaps a deeply heartfelt and charismatic personality that has the power to influence people to receive the charismatic spirit. If you were a born-again Baptist, you might consider true spirituality to be an abiding sense of God's presence in your life, such as when you first accepted Christ.

If you were a member of a liberal church, you might consider true spirituality to be a deep love for humanity, the kind of love that might drive you to help the downtrodden in your community or perhaps take a mission trip to help some village in South America cope with health issues or learn good farming methods.

If you lived in an African village and practiced a native religion, you might point to the village witch doctor as the most spiritual person around. If you were in a traditional American Indian community, you might point to the town animistic healer as quite spiritual. If you lived in a house with six of your friends, you might single out a girl who thought more deeply about things of the spirit and always raised difficult questions.

This list is not an attempt to categorize levels or types of spirituality but only to point out that the term *spiritual* is used for any number of things. And in some circles it has become watered down to the point that it means nothing more than that people are deeply interested in things of the intangible part of their being, their spirits, in preference to their bodies. Their spirituality is often an attempt to transcend their bodies and, as in the case of Buddhism, for example, to transcend pain and suffering.

So what is true spirituality? Most important, how would God define the term *spiritual?* What does Paul mean when he says that if we walk by the Spirit, we will not fulfill the desires of the flesh? What is the goal of true spirituality?

In the last two chapters, we have listened to Paul explain why we should live as God wants us to live. Through Baptism we have died with Christ—died with him to sin. And we have risen pure and free from sin—risen to serve God in our new and perfect lives. Through faith ("obedience to the truth"), we have been freed from our former master, sin, and become slaves to another master who lives in us, the righteousness we have as a gift from Jesus. In both cases our new status is not something we have to grow into over time and with a good deal of effort. It is a status we have by faith. Dead in Christ and living new lives free from sin. That's what we are! Slaves to a new master, namely, the righteousness of Christ that lives in us. That is what we are! It's a new status, just like a pauper who inherits a multimillion-dollar corporation has a new status. Our new status implies, yes, demands, a new life.

In Romans 7:1-6 Paul continues with one more explanation of our new status in Christ. This is another piece of knowledge of which he wants to remind us. It explains much about how we are to look at ourselves as God's people and what guides and motivates our lives. Paul paints a picture. Then he will apply it to us.

> Do you not know, brothers—for I am speaking to men who know the law—that the law has authority over a man only as long as he lives? For example, by law a married woman is bound to her husband as long as he is alive, but if her husband dies, she is released from the law of marriage. So then, if she marries another man while her husband is still alive, she is called an adulteress. But if her husband dies, she is released from that law and is not an adulteress, even though she marries another man. (Romans 7:1-3)

The picture is clear enough. All laws created on earth, whether created by man or by God, apply to a person only as long as that person is alive. A dead person is no longer accountable for keeping laws. A dead person is dead to the law.

Paul now applies this basic idea to you and me. He says:

> So, my brothers, you also died to the law through the body of Christ, that you might belong to another, to him who was raised from the dead, in order that we might bear fruit to God. (Romans 7:4)

Remember, we died with Christ. When Christ died, we died with him. When he rose, we rose with him. We were joined with Christ in his death so that we might rise and belong to him in his life. Of course, someday we will rise to live with the Lord eternally. In this section of Romans, however, Paul is talking about our time on earth and why we should live our lives in service to God. He stresses this and tells us why the Lord blessed us by joining us with Christ's death and resurrection: "in order that we might bear fruit to God."

Now comes the heart of the passage, the point to which Paul has been leading us:

> For when we were controlled by the sinful nature, the sinful passions aroused by the law were at work in our bodies, so that we bore fruit for death. But now, by dying to what once bound us, we have been released from the law so that we serve in the new way of the Spirit, and not in the old way of the written code. (Romans 7:5,6)

From the standpoint of how and why we live for God, this is one of the most powerful passages in Scripture. It takes us deeply into the meaning of the gospel and clearly explains what Jesus did for us. It is one of the most pointed explanations of Jesus' words "I am the vine; you are the branches. If a man remains in me and I in him, he will bear much fruit; apart from me you can do nothing" (John 15:5).

A couple simple illustrations may help. Imagine you are working as a secretary at a company. This company has a very thick handbook. You are accountable for literally thousands of rules and regulations. Imagine that your boss is very demanding. At every meeting he hauls out the handbook and reads some sections. He issues a stream of memos about this or that regulation. At every opportunity he drops hints that the company will be cutting back on staff, and the main criteria for choosing who goes and who stays is compliance with the rules and regulations of the handbook. Workers are urged to report fellow workers who commit infractions. When he finds someone not following the handbook, he hauls that person into his office and gives him or her a lecture, even if he or she didn't realize the regulation existed.

Now imagine another company. Your boss is one of the kindest people you know. Staff meetings are times of encouragement. Workers are urged to support their fellow workers. They know they won't be laid off. Work performance is judged in a spirit of love and respect. In this company the handbook is equally large, but it is kept in the company library for reference should someone need it. Surprisingly, you will often see employees in the library poring over the handbook because they have a question about policy and want to please their boss.

You get the picture, don't you? An employee in the first company is driven by fear. There is no possible way he or she could follow the rules and regulations of the handbook. Ignorance of the rules and the inability to be perfect dominate the workplace. Those who come closer to keeping the rules become proud and judgmental of the others. New employees cower in fear. But an employee in the second company is "free from the law" and lives in an environment of love and care. Employees seek out the handbook when they are confused about what they should do. They enjoy an environment with a caring boss and supportive fellow workers. In short, the employee in the first company serves "in the old way of the written code," and the employee in the new company serves "in the new way of the Spirit."

Let's try another picture and see if it helps. Mother bakes cookies on a regular basis to keep the cookie jar filled to the top. Once in a while she dispenses a cookie or two to one of her children or to a visitor. Imagine you are a little boy or girl, one of the family, who passes that cookie jar every day. Imagine you are quite young and you just take the cookie jar for granted, knowing that when your mother wants to, she will give you a cookie. You are quite content with the situation.

Now imagine that one morning you get up, go down to the kitchen, and above the cookie jar there is a big sign that reads:

DO NOT TAKE ANY COOKIES.

DO NOT TAKE EVEN ONE COOKIE.

DO NOT TOUCH THE COOKIES.

IF YOU DO, I WILL FIND YOU AND PUNISH YOU.

DO NOT EVEN THINK ABOUT TAKING A COOKIE BECAUSE
    I AM YOUR MOTHER AND I CAN READ MINDS AND
    I WILL PUNISH YOU IF YOU EVEN THINK ABOUT
    TAKING A COOKIE.

LOVE, MOM

Now the dynamic changes. You may not even have thought of taking a cookie, but now your mind is consumed with the thought. Maybe I won't get caught, you think. After all, I can just rearrange the cookies and make the jar look as full as it was before. But then you think of the last command: don't even think about it. You know you are "dead meat" because that's what you just did, thought about it.

The day wears on. All you find yourself thinking about is taking a cookie. You are consumed by the sign that told you not to take one. Maybe it's for my own good, you think. That helps for a while, but you find yourself still thinking about taking a cookie. I will just have to force myself not to think about the cookie jar, you say to yourself. You block the thought out of your mind for a while, but all of a sudden it rushes back into your consciousness. "Why did Mom do that?" you think. "Boy, has she gotten mean! I don't even want to see her tonight."

You get off the bus later in the afternoon. You slowly walk into the house. Mom is not around. You're going to take a cookie. You can't think of the punishment. You don't even think about the taste of the cookie. You just want one. Why? Because Mom said you couldn't have one. It sounds illogical. You can't explain your feelings. But you can't deny them either. You sneak in the back door and take a quick look to see if Mom is in the kitchen. She's not there. You slowly turn your eyes to the cookie jar and the sign. But look! Mom tore down the sign. Just a couple torn scraps of paper stuck to the cupboard door with the tape is all that is left of Mom's sign.

Now the situation changes again. The intense desire to steal a cookie is subsiding. The cookie jar looks like it used to look, a nice place where Mom stores cookies. Mom walks in. "Oh," she says, "I took down that sign. You can have a cookie whenever you want, but be good and don't eat too many." You happily grab a cookie and go off to do your homework. No fear, no punishment, no sin, no hatred.

Before we came to faith, we, like that child, were consumed with desire to disobey God. We were slaves to the sinful nature, controlled by it. It was a fire smoldering in our hearts. When God's laws came to mind, they were like gas thrown on that fire. We sinned, if not in our actions, then in our thoughts.

When we came to faith, we died with Christ and we died "to what once bound us," namely, the law. It has no part of our existence as God's people. It plays no role in our eternal life. It plays no role in our receiving God's blessings. It does not motivate us to serve God. Thankfully, it no longer makes our sinful nature jump into action. Why? Because in Christ, God has torn down the law. "Christ is the end of the law so that there may be righteousness for everyone who believes" (Romans 10:4).

Sad to say, this is a radical concept to many Christians. To many church members, Christianity means exactly the opposite. It means becoming more in touch and in tune with God's laws and, somehow or other, getting some supernatural help to keep them. But this is the opposite of what Paul says here. The supernatural help God gives to make us able to serve him is ours because he took us out from under the law. This act of God in Christ gives us the power to serve God because this alone quiets our sinful nature. Only when the fuel is gone does the fire go out. When the fuel of the law is taken away, the fire of the sinful nature goes out.

This is part of our faith. We believe it to be true. This is a key element of living by faith, not by sight. Everything I see around me in the world tells me that if I want something, I must earn it. Everything in life is tied to some kind of law, some type of cause-and-effect principle. If I am good, then . . . —you fill in the blank. We even experience the harmful effects of going against God's law. That is our experience!

But in Christ, a completely unheard of way of doing things is introduced. We need to listen to someone like Paul explain it to us. It is one aspect of the foolishness of the cross (1 Corinthians 1:18). When you hear that the law has no place in your life as a child of God, take it at face value. Don't try to qualify it in some way. Don't say, "Yes, but the commandments are still important, aren't they?" or "Paul bases many of his teachings on the law, doesn't he?" or "I can't neglect God's will, can I?" Yes, there is truth in those statements. But they must never in any way keep you from accepting what Paul says in this section of Romans 7. We died to what once bound us. We have been released from the law. We do not serve in the old way of the written code (the law). There is only one way the sinful nature can be stopped. You must take away its fuel. You must relegate the handbook to its proper place. You must tear down the sign above the cookie jar. In Christ, there is no law. He did away with it when he fulfilled it in his life and satisfied God's punishment on lawbreakers in his death. And you have been joined to him in death. You are dead to the law just as a married man is dead to the laws of marriage when he dies. Since you are resting in Christ and dead to the law, your sinful nature will rest too, and you will indeed serve God. "Live by the Spirit [who has joined you to Christ], and you will not gratify the desires of the sinful nature" (Galatians 5:16). That is not a command. It is a fact. This is not a method of motivation. This is a fact that has as much power over my sinful nature as I have over my campfire when I kick around the coals and douse them with a bucket of water.

In biblical terms, this is what true spirituality means. It is not something we generate in ourselves; it is not simply being concerned about things of the spirit as opposed to things of the body; it is not receiving some good-feeling spirit. It is having God's Spirit living in us, leading us to Christ, freeing us from the law, and for the first time in our lives, quieting our sinful nature and enabling us to serve God willingly. This is good news.

Before we conclude this chapter of our book, let's take a quick look at the rest of Romans 7. You see, at this point a couple problems arise. You and I have been listening to Paul tell us about the new life in service to righteousness that the Holy Spirit has worked in our hearts. The first problem that arises is that we look at ourselves and see a lot of evidence to the contrary. Our sinful natures are not dead. In fact, they are rather active, using the law as a springboard to sin. What does this mean in the context of everything we have just heard? Second, we hear Paul telling us to follow God's will. If we are truly serving God in the new way of the Spirit, you would think Paul wouldn't have to tell us to follow God's will. We would be doing it automatically. So what's the matter with us? Or what is the matter with God's Holy Spirit? Paul anticipates these thoughts, and in the last half of Romans 7, he gives us, as Paul Harvey would say, "the rest of the story."

The point Paul makes can be summarized like this: "Yes, we have the Holy Spirit working in us. His work is perfect and complete. We too are perfect and complete in Christ— completely forgiven and completely able to control the sinful nature. Don't ever think that you are less than God has made you in Christ, or that the Holy Spirit has worked in you a less than perfect new spirit. However, just as the Spirit working in you through the gospel is perfect, so the sinful nature you have in yourself is perfect as well—perfectly evil.

When Paul looks at himself, he does not see his old self gradually improving, or changing, into a new self. That's how we often think about growth in faith. We think we gradually change from being wicked to being righteous, like the sky changes from black to brilliant blue as the sun rises and dominates the sky. That may be how it appears on the surface, but under the skin things are happening a little differently. When Paul views himself, he sees two personalities, his old sinful nature and his new spiritual nature, understood as he has described it in Romans 7:1-6. These two personalities are continually fighting it out. Paul described the same spiritual battle when he wrote to the Galatians: "The sinful nature desires what is contrary to the Spirit, and the Spirit what is contrary to the sinful nature. They are in conflict with each other, so that you do not do what you want" (5:17).

At this point you might want to read Romans 7:7-13. There Paul describes what he observes the sinful nature doing in his person. The pictures in the previous paragraphs are drawn from what Paul says in those verses. The law is good. But the problem lies with our sinful nature, which takes the law and uses it as its tool to commit sin. When the law says, "You shall not," the sinful nature says, "You've just taught me another way to sin. Try and stop me."

Paul says that the law is spiritual (Romans 7:14). It can only be kept by a person who is spiritual too, that is, someone who has the will and desire and power to serve God freely and completely. But Paul says he, and we, cannot do that, for we are unspiritual. His sinful nature is still there, leading him to do the opposite of what he wants to do "in the new way of the Spirit." Read Romans 7:14-25a. See the struggle—constant and relentless—that is going on in Paul. His final conclusion about himself—yes, as a Christian—is this: "So then, I myself in my mind [because I am free from the law] am a slave to God's law, but in the sinful nature a slave to the law of sin" (verse 25). Depressing? Yes and no. Complete victory will be ours only in heaven. But it is better to know the enemy than to not know him, for if we know who he is, we are in a better position to defeat him.

Using the picture we introduced of the sky changing from black to brilliant blue, we might describe ourselves like this. But don't think of yourself as the sky changing its hues. Rather, think of yourself as both the blackest night and the sun in all its brilliance. As the sun rises in the sky, it becomes more and more dominant. It chases the darkness away. The darkness is not gone, and if the sun stops shining, the darkness will return as dark as it was before. But as long as the sun shines, it has its way, and the world is bathed in light.

In this life you will never be rid of the darkness of your sinful nature. But the sun of your new nature, which wants to serve God in true spirituality, is always there too (unless we shut Christ out of our hearts). Our goal is to have the sun shine more and more. It is to have the Holy Spirit more and more in control of our lives. How does this happen? Through the gospel alone. Only when we remind ourselves that we died and rose again with Christ are we inspired and motivated to not let sin reign in our bodies. Only when we know that our master is righteousness will we want to become more holy in our lives. Only when we know that we are dead to the law will we be able to serve God with a new, willing spirit. Only when we know and rehearse these truths can we admit with Paul's cold and brutal insight this truth about ourselves: "In the sinful nature [I am] a slave to the law of sin" (Romans 7:25). We can do that without flinching. For something much greater is working in us, the Spirit of Jesus Christ. Through his witness in our hearts, we have become truly spiritual.

5

The Gospel of a New Creation

When Christians are caught up in a sin or when they real-ize they are not living as God wants them to live, they ask themselves, "How can I change? How can I conform my life to God's will? How can I stop committing this sin?" People ask-ing those questions know God forgives all their sins, and they find comfort from the message of forgiveness. Christians know that God will give them the strength to overcome sin. They may read books to help them in their resolve, and they may try techniques to help themselves resist. They may read the Bible for hours on end, and they may meditate on the forgive-ness they find in the Lord's Supper.

Yet all the time they wonder why they have not improved. God works in mysterious ways, and perhaps time spent in defeat over some sin is God's way of curbing an even greater sin, the sin of pride that lurks below the surface in all of us. Yet perhaps lack of victory over sin comes because people do not really mine the depths of God's Word to discover the gospel in all its breadth and depth. Perhaps those people are focusing too much on their lack of performance for God than on the vast spectrum of God's performance for them.

Let's take this thought one step further. Perhaps a Christian has heard all that God has done for him or her but has not really savored what God has made of him or her. Lutherans focus on God's verdict of not guilty, justification, as the heart of the gospel, and rightly so. That is where everything begins. They are often afraid to emphasize Christ dwelling in us, and sometimes rightly so, because of all the talk we hear about the experience of "receiving Christ into your life" that has dominated many Christians' lives.

Preaching and teaching exclusively about God's love and forgiveness may not be the worst error a teacher can commit, but we come up short when we do not go further and delve into what that means in the Christian's being, that is, what it means not only before the throne of God but for the Christian's own inner life. Having said that, we must be completely clear that if talk about what we have become in Christ in any way clouds over an emphasis on God's forgiveness in Christ, then we will lose both. But where we are grounded in the substitutionary work of Jesus on the cross, we can, indeed we must, go on and talk about what we have become in him. This is not talk about what we should do for God but what we have become in Christ, which is a reality just as certain as Christ's death on the cross for us and the forgiveness we have because of his death.

This is gospel motivation as powerful and important as any. It is what Paul talks about in Romans 6 through 8. After he has talked about what Christ has done for us (3:21 through the end of chapter 5), Paul reminds us what Christ's victory has done in us, that is, what it has made us to be and given us the power to do. This is not a call to serve God because of what he has done for us. It is telling us how our lives are completely bound up in the gospel. Woven throughout this discussion are encouragements to live as we, in fact, *are* in Christ.

The Christian asks, "How can I change? How can I conform my life to God's will? How can I stop committing this sin?" Paul tells us, "In Christ, you are already doing that. In Christ, you have become a perfect person, a new creation, a person who is serving God in a perfect way." "Nonsense," you say, "I'm a first-class sinner." "But look here," Paul says, "in Baptism you died with Christ and rose with him. Your sinful nature was crucified with him, and you are living a life that is dead to sin and alive to God. You are just as perfect as Jesus was when he rose from the dead, for you rose along with him. And think further," Paul says. "When you came to faith, you were filled with Christ's righteousness. That became your master, and you are serving that master right now. It replaced the horrible master of sin. But there is more," Paul reminds us. "When you died and rose with Christ, you died to the law's demands—all of them—and right now you are serving the Lord in the new way of the Spirit, with a free heart. That's a fact. You are perfect!"

"So why do I sin?" you ask. Paul answers: "Because you still have a sinful nature that can't do anything but sin. It is perfectly rotten. I know, because I too have a sinful nature. But never lose sight of what you are. When I think of you, dear Christian, that's what I see, a perfect being in Christ. And God thinks of you that way too. Take the parts of your body that you are still yielding to sin, and use them in ways that are appropriate for a person who has died and risen from the dead. Take the sinful thoughts and actions, the ones your former master dictated, and get rid of them. Listen to what your new master, righteousness, dictates. And remember that you are free from the law, and your sinful nature has nothing to fan it into flame. Enjoy having it off your back, and do the kind of things your God wants you to do."

That's good news. It's good news about a new being, a new creation God has made of us, which has the power to serve God. Too often we Christians speak in generalities. We say, "Trust in God's grace and he will give you strength to overcome sin." True enough. But how? And when? And on what conditions? Paul does not speak in generalities. How do you overcome sin? Through what Christ has made you to be.

When? When you were baptized and right now as you believe in Christ. Conditions? None, other than remembering that you died with Christ and rose with him, that you are filled with Christ's righteousness and are a slave to that righteousness, that you are no longer under law, and that your sinful nature rests in inactivity.

That's good news, good news of a new creation. Paul's words speak to us new creations, giving shape to what we already know as recipients of God's forgiveness, letting us see clearly what we are, and through that clarity, giving us a rock-solid basis on which to serve the Lord. He tells us not to do something for God out of thanks for his love; he tells us what God has made us to be through his love. There is no "ought to" here. There is only the fact of what we, who are joined to the vine by faith, are doing now. There is no talk of what we potentially can do *if*. There is only talk of what we are already doing *because*.

We return to our discussion of Romans 6 through 8. Paul concluded chapter 7 by spelling out that he is a new creation living in a body decimated by sin: "So then, I myself in my mind am a slave to God's law, but in the sinful nature a slave to the law of sin" (7:25). That almost sounds like a cold, clinical analysis of what he is until we focus on two phrases: "I myself in my mind" and "in the sinful nature." Paul's real being is not his sinful nature but the new creation God has made of him. That is good news. You see, it's not a toss-up as to which side God will judge on the Last Day. God sees Paul for who he really is in Christ and will judge Paul on that basis. That is what Paul now explains in roughly the first half of chapter 8.

As you read Romans 8, keep in mind that Paul is describing what we are in Christ—new creations. In a way consistent with all of Scripture, Paul is saying that we new creations have nothing to fear, for we are not condemned. God is looking at our lives not from the standpoint of the forgiveness and righteousness we have in Christ but from the standpoint of the new life at work in us because of Christ's righteousness and forgiveness. We are not condemned because "the law of the Spirit of life," that is, the principle that through the Spirit I am a new being alive in service to God, has set me free from "the law of sin and death," that is, the principle that my sinful nature will always be stirred into action by the law, doing things that lead to death. In other words, the good news that we are not condemned is linked to what we have become in Christ.

How did this freedom come about? Not through the law. For although the law is good, it could only inflame the sinful nature into action; it could never make it inactive. So how do we become free from the law of sin and death? God sent his Son, who became like us and condemned sin in his own body. He did this by bearing our sin on himself and then taking it away through his sufferings and death. He did this by fulfilling the law. He did this by joining us to himself in his death and resurrection. Once we were joined with him, our sinful nature lost its power, as Paul has already explained. Now we live a completely righteous life through the "Spirit of life." The righteous requirements of the law are met in us, for we are walking according to the Spirit of life. And so we are not condemned. God sees in us what he is doing in us through his Spirit, the Spirit who has given us life in Jesus' death and resurrection. What our sinful nature is doing has no say in God's verdict on our lives.

Paul expands on this basic thought. Whether or not we are related to God as his sons and daughters depends on who is the guiding principle in our lives. If the real "me" is the sinful nature, I am lost. Why? Because the sinful nature can do nothing to please God. It does not—it cannot—submit to God's law. It is hostile to God. It leads to death. On the other hand, the mind controlled by the Spirit is life and peace. It is bound up with Christ's new life in service to God; it submits to God's will because Christ's righteousness has become its new master; it is alive in service to God because the law, which can only make us greater sinners, is no longer in the picture. Here there is life, and because there is life, there is peace.

We know God has established peace with us through Jesus' bloodshed on the cross. But can we link peace with our new life in Christ? We can, as long as we never separate our new life in Christ from what we have received from Christ through faith. In verse 9 Paul reminds us that we indeed are controlled by the Spirit, if the Spirit lives in us. (There is a bit of a warning in the last half of verse 9. If we reject the Spirit, we have completely lost all of these blessings.)

See what that means for us? If Christ is in us, we are alive because we have his righteousness, which gives life to our spirits and makes us free to serve the Lord. If Christ is in us, even our dead mortal bodies, which sin uses as its instruments, will be raised to life. These are the blessings we have because the law of the Spirit of life has set us free from the law of sin and death.

Now following the pattern he established in Romans 6, Paul encourages us in our lives of service to God. "We have an obligation," he says. To what? To the Spirit who is living in us. By nature we think we have an obligation to the sinful nature. We think about how we can please the sinful nature—with greed, lust, ambition, anger, and sinful pleasure. And by nature we spend our time planning how to pay our obligation to the flesh. But when we consider what it means that the Spirit is living in us, leading us to love and serve our Lord, and when we consider the outcome of this way of life, we must think differently. We have an obligation to the Spirit, as Paul says in Galatians 5:25: "Since we live by the Spirit, let us keep in step with the Spirit."

In Romans 8 Paul ties everything together:

> If you live according to the sinful nature, you will die; but if by the Spirit you put to death the misdeeds of the body, you will live, because those who are led by the Spirit of God are sons of God. For you did not receive a spirit that makes you a slave again to fear, but you received the Spirit of sonship. And by him we cry, "*Abba,* Father." The Spirit himself testifies with our spirit that we are God's children. (8:13-16)

Verses 13 and 14 are key. They link our lives of service to God (fulfilling our obligation to the Spirit) with our eternal life. If we are led by the Spirit, then we are children of God. Only then. The two go hand in hand.

We know that eternal life is ours as a gift of God's grace (Romans 6:23). We know eternal life comes through the forgiveness of sins won by Christ's sacrifice on the cross (3:24,28). We know we are saved by faith alone (4:4-8). But we must also realize the dynamic, if we might call it that, of what God's gracious gifts have done in our minds and hearts. The perfect service that we carry out through the Spirit of life is no less a reality than God's forgiveness of our sins. It is no less a part of God's grace than Jesus' death and resurrection for us.

It is interesting to note that for the first time in the book of Romans, Paul speaks about us as children of God. He did not do this when he proclaimed the gospel in chapters 3 to 5. He does it only now when he speaks of the Spirit working in us. The Spirit of life who is at work in us is also the one who assures us that we have been adopted by God and are now his children. And so where do our loyalties lie? To the flesh or to the Spirit of Christ living in us? Whom should we serve, the flesh whose deeds end in death or the Spirit who has joined us to Christ, created us to be new creatures living in service to God? The answer is obvious.

The good news that we are new creations, and a complete discussion of what this means, is essential to gospel motivation. Too often we jump from what Christ has done for us to what we *should* do for God. Too often we tell about God's love and then encourage one another to respond to that love by loving him in return. This is not wrong. What is wrong is to overlook that middle element that Paul uses as his foundation for teaching about service to God, namely, the firm reality of the new creation each of God's people has become. We have an obligation to God's love and forgiveness, but we also have an obligation to live according to the Spirit of life that is at work in us by virtue of God's love and forgiveness.

There almost seems to be a contradiction here: we *do* serve God; we *ought to* serve God. In other words, if we do serve God under the impulse of the Spirit of life, why does Paul need to tell us that we *should* yield ourselves in service to God? I cannot explain it logically, but I know it is true, as do all God's people. The sinful nature is still there. I still follow its prompting, even though I don't want to. I need to be reminded of who I really am, what I really am, and what I am now doing through the Spirit dwelling in me. I need to be reminded that the Spirit has led me and know that I am adopted by God as his child and how life in the Spirit will finally conclude. And then I need to be reminded of my obligation to shape my life according to what I already am. Illogical? Perhaps. But it is the logic of a believer's experience and also the logic Paul uses in Romans 8.

If we understand what Paul says in Romans 8, we will understand everything else he says about the new creation we have become in Christ. In 2 Corinthians 5:15-17 Paul wrote:

> **He died for all, that those who live** *should no longer live for themselves* but **for him who died for them and was raised again.** So from now on we regard no one from a worldly point of view. Though we once regarded Christ in this way, we do so no longer. **Therefore, if anyone is in Christ, he is a new creation; the old has gone, the new has come!**

We no longer think of people as the world does. The world knows only service to the sinful nature. It understands doing good only if there is something in it for the doer. It understands only greed, lust, and political maneuverings. It understands only the craving for recognition. In fact, that is how Paul once analyzed Jesus Christ, and in misguided zeal, he persecuted believers in Jesus for it. But when Paul came to know Christ, and be known by Christ, he realized how wrong he was. He came to understand there were vastly different motivations—a vastly different spirit—at work in Christ and his followers. He came to understand the new creation God's people are through the Spirit of life and how vastly different that is from what they were before.

In Galatians 6 Paul writes:

> Neither circumcision nor uncircumcision means anything; what counts is a new creation. (verse 15)

The sinful nature has its own way of thinking about one's relationship with God. A relationship with God, it thinks, must be based on keeping the law. Many Jewish Christians in Paul's day taught that non-Jews who wanted to become Christians had to be circumcised. Others shot back, saying that uncircumcision was the way to go, since we are free from Jewish regulations. Yet their way of thinking was as much bound up by the law as the former. None of this matters, writes Paul. All that matters is a new creation, a new being created by the gospel that loves and serves God in freedom prompted by the Spirit.

Paul speaks about the new creation in other terms. In Romans 12:2 he writes:

> Do not conform any longer to the pattern of this world, but be transformed by the renewing of your mind. Then you will be able to test and approve what God's will is—his good, pleasing and perfect will.

The word *mind* refers to the new creation. (See Romans 7:25.) At this point in Romans, Paul is about to launch into his instructions on everyday living. However, even though he will spend several chapters telling the Romans what they are to do, he begins by telling them to be renewed in their minds. In the context of Romans 7 and 8 this can mean nothing else than that we are to remember all that God has done for us and come to understand the new life these truths have created in us. Once we do that, we will have the foundation for determining what is God's will for our lives. We will understand love, his love for us and ours for our fellowman, and love will lead us in determining God's will. True knowledge of God's will does not start with the law but with the gospel, for the gospel alone renews our minds, enables us to love, and gives the Holy Spirit free reign in our hearts to produce the fruits of faith.

Paul speaks about the new creation again:

> *Do not lie to each other*, **since you have taken off your old self with its practices and have put on the new self,** which is being renewed in knowledge in the image of its Creator. (Colossians 3:9,10)

> Therefore we do not lose heart. Though outwardly we are wasting away, yet inwardly we are being renewed day by day. (2 Corinthians 4:16; note the King James translation: "For which cause we faint not; but though our outward man perish, yet the inward *man* is renewed day by day.")

63

The new creation is a perfect creation. The Spirit of life working in us is perfect in every way, perfect in zeal and perfect in knowledge. But Paul can also talk about the new self as being in the process of renewal day by day. How does this renewal take place? It takes place as Paul has described it in Romans 6 to 8—through the gospel of Jesus' death and resurrection, his gift of righteousness, and our release from the law. The sufferings we endure because of our faith wreak havoc with our outward body, either physically or emotionally. We see only death in the offing. But through this we are driven again and again to our Savior and, in the process, are renewed through the Spirit.

True renewal only comes through the gospel, for only the gospel provides the knowledge we need to be led by the Spirit of life. Only the gospel provides the basis on which the Spirit can create new creatures and keep those creations alive. Only the gospel provides the message of Christ's work *for us,* which has led to Christ's work *in us,* and lays on us the obligation to serve God, which we are most willing to fulfill. Any talk about renewal must center on Christ and only on Christ. When the law predominates, renewal ceases, for the Spirit is lost.

The writer to the Hebrews, quoting from Jeremiah 31:31-34, contrasts the covenant of the law with the promise of the gospel:

> The time is coming, declares the Lord, when I will make a new covenant with the house of Israel and with the house of Judah. It will not be like the covenant I made with their forefathers when I took them by the hand to lead them out of Egypt, because they did not remain faithful to my covenant, and I turned away from them, declares the Lord. This is the covenant I will make with the house of Israel after that time, declares the Lord. I will put my laws in their minds and write them on their hearts. I will be their God, and they will be my people. No longer will a man teach his neighbor, or a man his brother, saying, "Know the Lord," because they will all know me, from the least of them to the greatest. For I will forgive their wickedness and will remember their sins no more. (Hebrews 8:8-12)

The phrase "I will put my laws in their minds and write them on their hearts" refers to the creation of the new man. What the law was powerless to do, using Paul's phrase, God did by forgiving "their wickedness" and remembering "their sins no more." No longer would they be forced to live according to a set rule of laws and have to teach one another the laws (even though those laws were right and good and filled with pictures of God's future salvation). That didn't work; for as Paul explains, the law only fuels the sinful nature and gives us reason to sin. Rather, God simply forgave their sins, and with that message of forgiveness came the Holy Spirit and a new way of serving the Lord.

Dear Christian, realize what a wonderful thing it is that right now you are a new creature, made that way through being joined with Christ. Through the Spirit, you are—right now—putting to death the misdeeds of the body.

6

The Gospel of How God Views New Creations

God has made us new creations by uniting us with Jesus' death and resurrection, by giving us the gift of righteousness, and by releasing us from the law. We are now alive. Why are we now alive? Paul explains why in Romans 8:13: Through the Spirit we can and are putting to death the misdeeds of the body. We are doing this because we have in us the Spirit of Christ, whom we have received by faith. The Spirit has made us children of God by virtue of Christ's life, death, and resurrection. What we are as new creations is so intimately bound together with what Jesus has done for us that we cannot think of ourselves apart from his death and resurrection.

We are not saved by what we do, nor are we saved *because* we are serving the Lord. However, Scripture often describes our relationship with God and our hope of eternal life in terms of what we are as new creatures. In other words, many sections of Scripture speak of the blessings we have in Christ as coming to us *because of what we do for God.*

This is one of the most wonderful ways Scripture encourages us to strive to serve the Lord. Scripture encourages us to remember our roots—Jesus' death and righteousness—and like branches growing out of the vine, to rejoice in the fruit we are producing and in the blessings we are receiving.

We have already focused on two of the passages that give this encouragement. In Romans 8:1 Paul told us that we in whom the Spirit of life is working are not condemned. Romans 8:13 spoke about the eternal life we have as people who, through the Spirit, put to death the misdeeds of the body. These truths—so closely tied with Jesus' cross and empty tomb—motivate us to give ourselves to the Lord.

These passages, though, are some of the most difficult passages in the New Testament. True Christians want nothing other than the comfort of knowing that they are free from sin and guilt and that they can be absolutely sure of eternal life. True Christians strive to hold on to the message of forgiveness as their only way to eternal life. The passages that speak of these blessings in terms of what we do might strike us as foreign. We might have trouble understanding them. Sometimes we ignore them. Sometimes we reinterpret them to fit easier passages that speak of God's blessings in terms of Jesus' grace and forgiveness. We do this because we do not want to fall into work-righteousness. The casual reader may jump to the conclusion that these passages, in fact, do teach righteousness by works. Not only casual readers but Christian scholars have interpreted these passages as teaching that God does not bless us by his grace alone but because we have earned his blessings with our good lives.

We must always remember the perfectly clear passages in the Bible about salvation by grace through faith in Christ's work for us. It should be impossible for us to misinterpret passages that promise God's grace and eternal life to those who obey the law. Yet so many do misinterpret these passages, twisting and turning them into obstacles to gospel motivation.

Our sinful nature willingly goes along with these misinterpretations, coming away with a spirit of despair over our inability to serve God well enough or a spirit of pride in the mistaken notion that we have kept God's commandments well enough to earn his grace.

In spite of the misinterpretations, the passages that link our new creation with God's blessings should not be ignored or reinterpreted. Properly understood, these passages encourage us to serve the Lord and are part of gospel motivation. We are what we are as God's people only because God has led us to believe the gospel of Jesus' death and resurrection. These passages rest on the truth of what Christ has made us to be. They help us view ourselves and our lives as the Lord wants us to view them. They help us appreciate what God has made us to be and what an important place our new lives play in God's will for his people.

Passages that link God's blessings to the fruits of our new creations are repeated throughout the New Testament in various ways. We must come to the point where we can speak as Scripture speaks, yet be content that we are not promoting work-righteousness. Again, Romans 8:12-16 has provided the key for doing this.

In this chapter of our book, we will look at passages that fall into three general categories: (1) We will look at passages that speak of *our relationship to God* in terms of how we live, that is, our good works. These passages encourage us to remain firm in our faith so that we can live in the Spirit and continually serve the Lord. (2) We will look at passages that speak of *eternal life* in terms of how we live. These passages also encourage us to remain firm in our faith so that as new creations we stand before God pure and holy in Christ. (3) We will look at passages that encourage us to persevere in *godly living* by reminding us that the Lord will reward the good we do.

Our relationship with God and our lives of service

Our relationship with God is based on what he has done for us in Christ, not on what we do for him. This is the heart of the gospel. Jesus died for the sins of the whole world, and we have come to faith in that fact. We are children of God through faith in the salvation he provided by his Son.

In the previous chapters, however, we saw that the gospel has made us into new people. We want to serve our Lord, and we can serve him. This is not an option. If I'm at the beach and about to pour water on someone, I don't say, "Watch out, you might get wet." I say, "Watch out, you're *going* to get wet." If I pour water on something, it *will* get wet. It can't help but get wet. When I come to faith in Christ, I can't help but serve him. I'm a new creation, created by the Spirit, and I fear and love God. It is true that I still sin, I still rebel, and I still covet. But that's only because my sinful nature is still struggling to exert control over my life. My sinful nature is not who I really am. The "real" me serves God in freedom and out of love. And so it is fair to speak of our relationship with God in terms of what we are as Christians.

Forgiveness

> *If you forgive men when they sin against you,* **your heavenly Father will also forgive you.** But if you do not forgive men their sins, your Father will not forgive your sins. (Matthew 6:14,15)

> When you stand praying, *if you hold anything against anyone, forgive him,* **so that your Father in heaven may forgive you your sins.** (Mark 11:25)

God forgives us when we, as believers in Christ, forgive those who sin against us. We don't earn his forgiveness, but if we refuse to forgive others, we have given up our faith. If we find it impossible to forgive others, it is clear that we find no need for God's forgiveness. If this is so, we have cut ourselves off from God's forgiveness. But if we forgive others, our faith in Christ is real and we receive his forgiveness.

Once Jesus was a dinner guest at the home of a Pharisee. During the meal a woman came in and anointed Jesus' feet with perfume and wiped his feet with her hair. Considering what a sinful life this woman had been living, Simon the Pharisee was amazed that Jesus was allowing her to do this:

Jesus answered him, "Simon, I have something to tell you." "Tell me, teacher," he said. "Two men owed money to a certain moneylender. One owed him five hundred denarii, and the other fifty. Neither of them had the money to pay him back, so he canceled the debts of both. Now which of them will love him more?" Simon replied, "I suppose the one who had the bigger debt canceled." "You have judged correctly," Jesus said. Then he turned toward the woman and said to Simon, "Do you see this woman? I came into your house. You did not give me any water for my feet, but she wet my feet with her tears and wiped them with her hair. You did not give me a kiss, but this woman, from the time I entered, has not stopped kissing my feet. You did not put oil on my head, but she has poured perfume on my feet. Therefore, I tell you, **her many sins have been forgiven**—*for she loved much.* But he who has been forgiven little loves little." (Luke 7:40-47)

The woman's many sins were forgiven. Why? Because she "loved much." Jesus was evaluating this woman's realization of how much she had been forgiven on the basis of how much love she showed him. Yet at the end of the section, Jesus reminds the woman that her faith in him saved her. "Jesus said to the woman, 'Your faith has saved you; go in peace'" (Luke 7:50).

Children of God

By what we do, we are seen to be like our Lord, and for that reason we will be called children of God:

> *Love your enemies, do good to them, and lend to them without expecting to get anything back.* **Then your reward will be great, and you will be sons of the Most High,** because he is kind to the ungrateful and wicked. *Be merciful,* **just as your Father is merciful.** (Luke 6:35,36)

When we love and bless our enemies, the Lord calls us his children. When he sees us showing mercy to others, he looks at us and thinks, "That's my boy" or "That's my girl." "He's a chip off the old block!" "She really takes after her dad!" We all know how encouraging it is to have our earthly parents say

such things to us. How wonderful it is to have our heavenly
Father speak like that to us!

Jesus' disciples

In another place, Jesus tells us that people know we are his
disciples because we love one another:

> A new command I give you: Love one another. **As I have
> loved you,** *so you must love one another.* By this all men
> will know that you are my disciples, if you love one another.
> (John 13:34,35)

People in whom Jesus lives

At the Last Supper, Jesus told his disciples that he would
reveal himself to them, but not to the world. One of Jesus' disciples could not understand how Jesus could do that. Notice
the progression of thought in Jesus' answer. You could take
Jesus' response as work-righteousness. But notice the encouragement to service that flows from what he says. When we
come to faith in Jesus, we serve him:

> Then Judas (not Judas Iscariot) said, "But, Lord, why do you
> intend to show yourself to us and not to the world?" Jesus
> replied, *"If anyone loves me, he will obey my teaching.* **My
> Father will love him, and we will come to him and
> make our home with him.** He who does not love me will
> not obey my teaching. (John 14:22-24)

This service, which comes from people who have become new
creations, is a sign of our love. Jesus promises that his Father
will love such people and that Jesus himself will come to us
and reveal his love to us in ever-increasing measure.

We remain in Jesus' love

Chapter 15 of John's gospel contains some of Jesus' most
well-known words. These words describe our relationship to
him. Notice how Jesus bases everything the disciples have
become on the Word he has spoken to them. They believed
that Word and were joined with him (think of Romans 6–8).

He encourages them to remain in him and in his love. The Father is glorified when we bear fruit and put on display our faith in his Son.

> I am the true vine, and my Father is the gardener. He cuts off every branch in me that bears no fruit, while every branch that does bear fruit he prunes so that it will be even more fruitful. You are already clean because of the word I have spoken to you. *Remain in me,* **and I will remain in you.** No branch can bear fruit by itself; it must remain in the vine. Neither can you bear fruit unless you remain in me. I am the vine; you are the branches. If a man remains in me and I in him, he will bear much fruit; apart from me you can do nothing. This is to my Father's glory, that you bear much fruit, showing yourselves to be my disciples. (John 15:1-5,8)

Now Jesus makes a comparison that no one but a Christian understands:

> As the Father has loved me, so have I loved you. Now remain **in my love.** *If you obey my commands, you will remain in my love,* just as I have obeyed my Father's commands and remain in his love. I have told you this so that my joy may be in you and that your joy may be complete. My command is this: *Love each other* **as I have loved you. Greater love has no one than this, that he lay down his life for his friends.** *You are my friends if you do what I command.* (John 15:9-14)

The Father loves Jesus. Jesus obeys the Father and remains in his love. Jesus loves us. We obey Jesus and remain in his love. The Father loved his Son and sent him into the world to accomplish our salvation. Humanly speaking, Jesus struggled, but he always had a willing spirit, and he completed his Father's work. He remained in his Father's love.

Our service is no different. Because we are joined with Christ in his death and resurrection, because we are slaves to righteousness, and because the law does not fan our sinful natures into flame any longer, our service is just as willing as Jesus' service was. Christians who know this—and all Christians do—will never view these words as an impossible command, an unrealistic expectation, or a harsh condition. It is no more or less than an encouragement to keep doing what Jesus has enabled us to do. This helps us realize what complete freedom there is in being new creatures in Christ.

Jesus told Nicodemus why believers come into his light:

> Whoever believes in him is not condemned, but whoever does not believe stands condemned already because he has not believed in the name of God's one and only Son. This is the verdict: Light has come into the world, but men loved darkness instead of light because their deeds were evil. Everyone who does evil hates the light, and will not come into the light for fear that his deeds will be exposed. But whoever lives by the truth comes into the light, so that it may be seen plainly that what he has done has been done through God. (John 3:18-20)

Jesus invited us to come into the light of his grace, and we have accepted his invitation. Our sins were forgiven, and we became new creatures. Jesus' point in these verses is that we are not ashamed to stand in the light of his glory because we are acting like him. We are not ashamed to stand under the light of his holiness because we have been freed from sin's power through the Spirit of life. According to our new man, we have nothing to hide from the scrutiny of his judgment. As Paul says in Romans 8:1, there is no condemnation for us who are in Christ Jesus. (Anyone who is afraid to come into his light has something to fear.) When believers come into the light, it is clear to them that they are serving the Lord in the Lord's own power, not theirs. Jesus' words never foster pride, only gratitude and humility. We bask in God's light because we are doing the good he is working in us.

We are righteous in Christ

The book of 1 John contains many similar statements. John weaves together what Jesus has done for us (that's always first) with the love we show to others. He joins the two so intimately that if we see the fruits of faith in our lives, particularly love, we can be sure we are children of God:

You know that he appeared so that he might take away our sins. And in him is no sin. No one who lives in him keeps on sinning. No one who continues to sin has either seen him or known him. Dear children, do not let anyone lead you astray. *He who does what is right* **is righteous, just as he [He] is righteous.** He who does what is sinful is of the devil, because the devil has been sinning from the beginning. The reason the Son of God appeared was to destroy the devil's work. No one who is born of God will continue to sin, because God's seed remains in him; he cannot go on sinning, because he has been born of God. This is how we know who the children of God are and who the children of the devil are: Anyone who does not do what is right is not a child of God; nor is anyone who does not love his brother. (1 John 3:5-10)

"God's seed" is simply another term for our new creation. The seed of the gospel has been planted in the believer's heart. That seed has become a plant. A plant must grow, or it will die. A plant must produce fruit; that's its nature. To live in sin and to keep on sinning is impossible for Christians; it goes against their nature. John says, "He who does what is right is righteous, just as he is righteous." The NIV translation might have capitalized "he." Jesus has been referred to as "he" in the preceding verses. The meaning is that if we do the right thing, it is clear that we are righteous in Christ.

God's love is complete in us

The next quotation from Scripture says that if we love, we can be sure of the following things: We have been born of God. We know God. God lives in us. The love God has for us has fulfilled its goal in us, that is, it has been "made complete in us." (This does not mean that our love is perfect.) So we live in God, and God lives in us.

> Dear friends, let us love one another, for love comes from God. *Everyone who loves* **has been born of God and knows God.** Whoever does not love does not know God, because God is love. This is how God showed his love among us: He sent his one and only Son into the world that we might live through him. This is love: not that we loved God,

> but that he loved us and sent his Son as an atoning sacrifice for our sins. Dear friends, **since God so loved us,** *we also ought to love one another.* No one has ever seen God; but *if we love one another,* **God lives in us and his love is made complete in us.** We know that we live in him and he in us, because he has given us of his Spirit. And we have seen and testify that the Father has sent his Son to be the Savior of the world. If anyone acknowledges that Jesus is the Son of God, God lives in him and he in God. And so we know and rely on the love God has for us. God is love. **Whoever lives in love lives in God, and God in him.** (1 John 4:7-16)

How can John link these great gifts to our love? The previous passages make it clear that everything begins with God's love for us in Christ. "We know and rely on the love God has for us." Our faith has overcome the world. We are free from guilt and will not stand condemned with the world on the Last Day.

We are also free from the power of sin, because, as John says in the following quotation, if we love God, we will (not will try to, but will) obey his commandments:

> This is how we know that we love the children of God: by loving God and carrying out his commands. *This is love for God: to obey his commands. And his commands are not burdensome,* **for everyone born of God overcomes the world.** This is the victory that has overcome the world, even our faith. Who is it that overcomes the world? Only he who believes that Jesus is the Son of God. (1 John 5:2-5)

A person who reads work-righteousness into the above passages is doing just that, reading his or her own thoughts into them. But anyone who ignores these passages, or who does not want to be drawn up into John's way of speaking, robs himself of many beautiful encouragements to value what God has made him to be—a person who can love. The gospel, which John weaves into his presentations, anchors us always on Christ's righteousness. Our love as evidence of our faith and as a source of God's blessings anchors us on how important our love is.

We will have peace with God on the Last Day

John links peace with God to the fact that we are new creations and live as such:

> Dear children, let us not love with words or tongue but with actions and in truth. This then is how we know that we belong to the truth, and how we set our hearts at rest in his presence whenever our hearts condemn us. For God is greater than our hearts, and he knows everything. Dear friends, if our hearts do not condemn us, **we have confidence before God and receive from him anything we ask,** *because we obey his commands and do what pleases him.* And this is his command: to believe in the name of his Son, Jesus Christ, and to love one another as he commanded us. *Those who obey his commands* **live in him, and he in them.** (1 John 3:18-24)

John tells us to love with our actions and in truth. When we do this, we know that we have faith in Christ. At times we question our faith. We feel guilty and uneasy in God's presence. Our hearts condemn us for our many sins. Yet when we look at the love we show in our lives, we see evidence that we are in the faith, and we can be at ease before God. What's more, God sees fruits of faith that our hearts don't see. He knows everything, our faith and the good works of our new man, which are sometimes hidden even to us. On the other hand, when we see ourselves producing the fruits of faith, we know that Christ, who died for us and has forgiven us, is dwelling in our hearts. And if that is so, there can be no doubt that God accepts us. We can confidently approach God's throne of grace. What's more, we receive answers to our prayers. Why? Because we obey him, first by believing in Christ and then by showing love to others as he has commanded us.

John weaves together faith in Christ, love for others, confidence before God, and certainty of faith. We might like to say that our certainty is found only in Christ's work for us. John is not so cut-and-dry. The fruits of faith—because they come from faith—also play into our certainty that we are in the faith and that God is at peace with us. John speaks no differently than Jesus speaks. Through statements like these, we are encouraged in faith and Christian living, and we realize how great a role our lives of faith play in our understanding of ourselves as God's people.

We will offer another quotation from 1 John at the beginning of the next section. But first let's look at a section of Scripture that has caused Christians a lot of trouble. Perhaps this section will be more clear in the context of the passages we have already looked at.

It is clear that we are justified

The apostle James was dealing with people who had fallen into the false belief that as long as they believed in Christ, doing good works in their lives was not important. Since they considered themselves righteous before God, they thought there was no need for righteousness in their lives. They considered themselves justified, but there was no evidence of that fact. So James made it clear to them that faith without works is dead:

> What good is it, my brothers, if a man claims to have faith but has no deeds? Can such faith save him? Suppose a brother or sister is without clothes and daily food. If one of you says to him, "Go, I wish you well; keep warm and well fed," but does nothing about his physical needs, what good is it? In the same way, faith by itself, if it is not accompanied by action, is dead. But someone will say, "You have faith; I have deeds." Show me your faith without deeds, and I will show you my faith by what I do. You believe that there is one God. Good! Even the demons believe that—and shudder. You foolish man, do you want evidence that faith without deeds is useless? Was not our ancestor Abraham considered righteous for what he did when he offered his son Isaac on the altar? You see that his faith and his actions were working together, and his faith was made complete by what he did. And the scripture was fulfilled that says, "Abraham believed God, and it was credited to him as righteousness," and he was called God's friend. You see that a person is justified by what he does and not by faith alone. (James 2:14-24)

James' point is simple. Faith without works is no faith at all. He proves this by going back into the Old Testament and citing the example of Abraham. Abraham, of course, is the most important example of faith in the Old Testament. Saint Paul spends much of Romans 4 talking about Abraham's faith. He points out that Abraham believed in God and that his faith is what made him righteous. Paul also points out that Abraham received the promise by faith "so that it may be by grace and may be guaranteed to all Abraham's offspring—not only to those who are of the law but also to those who are of the faith of Abraham" (Romans 4:16). Yet Abraham is also one of the best examples of a person who became a new creation by faith, showed to the Lord and to the world what the Lord had made him to be, and then was blessed by God on the basis of what he did.

We see this from Genesis 22 and 26. Up until Genesis 22, we hear nothing of Abraham's works as the reason God blessed him. God's blessings were promises, given to Abraham completely apart from anything he did. If nothing else, Genesis 12 through 21 make it clear that every single promise God gave to Abraham came by faith alone. In Genesis 22, however, these promises are spoken of for the first time as belonging to Abraham because of what he did. After Abraham nearly sacrificed his son Isaac, the Lord said to him, "Now I know that you fear God, because you have not withheld from me your son, your only son. . . . I will surely bless you . . . and through your offspring all nations on earth will be blessed, because you have obeyed me" (Genesis 22:12-18). The promises had not changed. Nor had God. His promises were still promises. But now God was linking the fulfillment of his promises to what Abraham did in faith. Later, when God passed on to Isaac the blessings he had given to Abraham, he put it this way: "I will make your descendants as numerous as the stars in the sky and will give them all these lands, and through your offspring all nations on earth will be blessed, because Abraham obeyed me and kept my requirements, my commands, my decrees and my laws" (Genesis 26:4,5). Here God's statement is even more pointed.

Rather than obscuring the matter, James clears up what would seem to be a rather difficult Old Testament passage. Abraham's faith was a living faith. Abraham was a new creation, made that way because of God's promises. No one could see Abraham's faith until God tested him. His faith burst forth in service, and God blessed his obedience. God saw his faith. The world saw his faith. Without works this would have been impossible. If Abraham had disobeyed God and refused to sacrifice Isaac, he would have been telling the world that he didn't believe; he would have forfeited the promises, and he would have been lost. But his faith was made complete by his works, that is, everything the Bible says about Abraham's faith is true because Abraham was a new creation, which became apparent at this time. In fact, when God transferred the promises to Isaac, he still had in mind the evidence of Abraham's faith and even tied his promises to Isaac with what Abraham had done by faith.

Although James is rebuking those whose faith, in many cases, was dead, his words are still motivation for us. We want to imitate Abraham. James describes what the Lord's promises had done in Abraham's heart. We ask the Lord to do the same in our hearts and continue to enable our faith to be complete by our works. If that does not happen, our faith is dead and we are dead to God's promises. But if that happens, we will be blessed.

Just to repeat: The above passages link our lives of service with the promises we normally associate with the gospel. But this is not work-righteousness. It is simply an encouragement to live in line with the righteousness we have in Christ, an encouragement to live according to our new man, which is there only because we know Jesus' forgiveness. Admittedly, some of these passages are difficult. Yet they are part of God's Word, meant not to trouble our faith but to spur us on to live our faith, which we can do because we are in Christ.

Our lives of service and eternal life

Scripture also ties our hope of eternal life to what we do. We return to 1 John and look at a section in which John speaks in these terms:

God is love. *Whoever lives in love* **lives in God, and God in him.** In this way, love is made complete among us so that **we will have confidence on the day of judgment,** *because in this world we are like him.* There is no fear in love. But perfect love drives out fear, because fear has to do with punishment. The one who fears is not made perfect in love. We love because he first loved us. If anyone says, "I love God," yet hates his brother, he is a liar. For anyone who does not love his brother, whom he has seen, cannot love God, whom he has not seen. (1 John 4:16-20)

John reminds us that God is love. If we live in love, then we are united with God and God with us. When this happens, God's love is made complete in us, that is, it is producing fruits of faith in our lives. When this happens, we can be confident on the day of judgment. Why? Because in this world we are like our Lord. We can look at ourselves and see people who are imitating God's love. Again, read all of this in the context of Romans 6 through 8. The power of the gospel is at work in our hearts. John reminds us that God loves us, and so our lives cannot help but reflect his love for us. If we see our hearts empty of love, we have every reason to fear the judgment, for if that is the case, we have given up our faith.

George Stoeckhardt, a great 19th century Lutheran Scripture commentator from the Missouri Synod, put it this way:

This is said [verse 17] of the love that is with us, that dwells in us. It is our love, which has its origin in God. This love has reached its end and purpose when it enables us to face Judgment Day with confidence. By this everyone can test himself whether he really possesses this love, as he considers in what frame of mind he approaches Judgment Day. Whoever has this God-born love is not frightened at the thought of Judgment Day. He approaches this Day with fearless confidence. He enters the presence of the great Judge unafraid. . . . We must remember that the Apostle at this place does not say how Christians, terrified about their sins, should meet the thought of Judgment Day. Only by faith in Christ, which apprehends the merits of Christ, can one stand before the Judge. That is here presupposed. From such faith necessarily flows love. That faith in Christ quiets our heart against sin, we have read earlier in this epistle.

> Yet, what the Apostle writes here is meant to test our faith. Are we terrified by the thought of Judgment! We ought not be. Our love is an evidence of faith. (*Lectures on the Three Letters of John,* translated by Hugo W. Degner. Atkin, Minnesota: Hope Press, 1963, pp. 107-109)

In light of how some confessional Lutheran commentators deal with passages like this, it is important to hear how Stoeckhardt simply lets the passage mean what the words say. What too often happens is that confessional Lutherans explain these passages by virtually ignoring the emphasis on works and basing everything on Christ's work for us. They do not take into consideration that through the gospel God has made us new creatures and that Scripture often bases God's rewards, now and in eternity, on what God has made us to be. Lutheran commentators can hardly be faulted for this. These passages are what all proponents of salvation by works have thrown in the faces of Lutherans for centuries, using these passages to "prove" that salvation does not come through faith alone but through works. Yet basing all God's blessings directly on Christ's work is undermining God's way of leading us into greater service. This is not a matter of forgetting Christ and focusing on works. Rather, it is a matter of acknowledging what an immediate impact Christ's work has and, of necessity, must have on our lives. It is acknowledging that in Christ we are serving God and that we have an obligation to our new nature to live according to it. And we are blessed if we carry out this obligation.

If these passages make you feel uneasy or seem to pull you back under the curse of the law, you are not understanding them correctly and I will take the blame for not explaining them as clearly as I could. But the issue is real. We must wrestle with the passages, drawing out their natural meaning from what the words say.

The key to understanding these passages is Romans 6 through 8. These chapters come after Paul has preached the clear message of salvation by faith in Jesus' work alone. They come after Paul has preached the objective nature of Jesus' work, that is, that his work on the cross covered the sins of all people. When Paul begins talking about sanctification, he does not forget about justification in Christ. Rather, he builds on it, showing its natural outgrowth in our becoming new people, new in our relation to God, new in our relationship to the law (we are free from it) because we now have Christ's righteousness (and are slaves to it). The gospel—our being grounded in Christ's righteousness and having a sure hope of eternal life in our Savior—is the end of the line when it comes to our hope. But it is not the end of the line. The gospel makes us new creations. Where there is no new creation, there is no salvation or any of the other blessings of God.

The key to understanding these passages is to know the gospel better and better. The more we know God's love and find our hope in his love alone, the less we will be tempted to turn these passages into law passages and the more we will be enabled to take them to heart in the way they were intended. The more we rest in the Savior, the more we will rejoice in the fact that we are new people in him and the more we will be able to fit these passages into our day-to-day lives as God's people.

The following passages also speak of God giving eternal blessings to those who, by faith, live for him. We will not comment on them. Simply read them in the context of what we have already discussed.

> **It will be good** *for those servants whose master finds them ready,* even if he comes in the second or third watch of the night. (Luke 12:38)

> The man who loves his life will lose it, *while the man who hates his life in this world* **will keep it for eternal life.** Whoever serves me must follow me; and where I am, my servant also will be. My Father will honor the one who serves me. (John 12:25,26)

> God "will give to each person according to what he has done." *To those who by persistence in doing good seek glory, honor and immortality,* **he will give eternal life.** But for those who are self-seeking and who reject the truth and follow evil, there will be wrath and anger. There will be trouble and distress for every human being who does evil: first for the Jew, then for the Gentile; but glory, honor and peace for everyone who does good: first for the Jew, then for the Gentile. For God does not show favoritism. (Romans 2:6-11)

> *I have fought the good fight, I have finished the race, I have kept the faith.* **Now there is in store for me the crown of righteousness,** which the Lord, the righteous Judge, will award to me on that day—and not only to me, but also to all who have longed for his appearing. (2 Timothy 4:7,8)

> Do not be deceived: God cannot be mocked. *A man reaps what he sows.* The one who sows to please his sinful nature, from that nature will reap destruction; the *one who sows to please the Spirit,* **from the Spirit will reap eternal life.** Let us not become weary in doing good, for **at the proper time we will reap a harvest** *if we do not give up.* (Galatians 6:7-9)

> Just as he who called you is holy, so be holy in all you do; for it is written: "Be holy, because I am holy." **Since you call on a Father who judges each man's work impartially,** *live your lives as strangers here in reverent fear.* **For you know that it was not with perishable things such as silver or gold that you were redeemed from the empty way of life handed down to you from your forefathers, but with the precious blood of Christ, a lamb without blemish or defect.** He was chosen before the creation of the world, but was revealed in these last times for your sake. (1 Peter 1:15-20)

Finally, Paul encourages the Corinthians to live with a view to eternal life:

> We make it our goal to please him, whether we are at home in the body or away from it. For we must all appear before the judgment seat of Christ, that each one may receive what is due him for the things done while in the body, whether good or bad. (2 Corinthians 5:9,10)

God's reward on our lives of service

Finally, let's look at passages that deal with rewards God gives us because we have served him. We call these rewards of grace because they are rewards that God graciously gives us because of the good works he has enabled us to perform by his Spirit through Christ.

Let me introduce a passage from one of Luther's writings. Luther was continually bombarded by false teachers who used passages that spoke of rewards as proof for their false teaching of salvation by works. This is a long quotation, but it clearly points out the problem and Luther's solution on how we should understand God's rewards. In his exposition on Matthew, Luther writes:

> The blind, false preachers conclude from these passages [such as 5:12: "The reward of those persecuted for His sake shall be great in heaven"] that we get to heaven and are saved by our work and labor, and on this then they found their chapter houses, cloisters, pilgrimages, masses, etc. . . . We must know the difference between grace and merit. Grace and merit do not accord with each other. If one preaches grace, he surely cannot preach merit; and whatever is grace cannot be merit, else grace, as St. Paul says, Romans 11:6, would not be grace. Whoever mixes these two confuses the people and leads both himself and his hearers astray. . . . But how, then, do you explain the many passages which speak of reward and merit? Of that we say to the common people that the promises of a reward are mighty consolations to the Christians. For after you have become a Christian and now have a gracious God and the remission of all your sins, both your past sins and those which you daily commit, you will find that you must do and suffer much because of your faith and Baptism. For the abominable devil in company with the world and the flesh will be on your trail and plague you on all sides, as Christ has shown sufficiently throughout these three chapters; you will feel as though there is no room left for you in the world. If, now, He would let us remain without a word of consolation, we would despair because of this persecution and say: Who wants to be a Christian, preach, and do good works? Is this to last eternally? Is it never going to change? Here He steps up to us, consoles, and strengthens us, and says: You are now in grace and God's children; although you must on that account suffer in the world, be not terrified, but be firm, do not permit these things to tire and weaken you, but let every man perform his duty; he may fare badly, but that shall not be his loss; let him know that the kingdom of heaven is his and that he shall be richly repaid for it. . . . Not that the works deserve it because of their worthiness, but because He has promised it for our strengthening and

consolation, that we might not think that our labor, burden, and misery were in vain and forgotten. (Francis Pieper, *Christian Dogmatics,* Volume III, St. Louis: Concordia Publishing House, 1953, pp. 57,58)

The following is a sample of the passages that speak about God rewarding us because of our lives. Again, simply read these passages in light of what we have discussed so far.

Blessed are you when people insult you, persecute you and falsely say all kinds of evil against you because of me. *Rejoice and be glad,* **because great is your reward in heaven,** for in the same way they persecuted the prophets who were before you. (Matthew 5:11,12)

Be careful not to do your "acts of righteousness" before men, to be seen by them. If you do, you will have no reward from your Father in heaven. So when you give to the needy, do not announce it with trumpets, as the hypocrites do in the synagogues and on the streets, to be honored by men. I tell you the truth, they have received their reward in full. But when you give to the needy, *do not let your left hand know what your right hand is doing, so that your giving may be in secret.* **Then your Father, who sees what is done in secret, will reward you.** (Matthew 6:1-4)

Everyone who has left houses or brothers or sisters or father or mother or children or fields for my sake **will receive a hundred times as much and will inherit eternal life.** (Matthew 19:29)

Then the King will say to those on his right, "**Come, you who are blessed by my Father; take your inheritance, the kingdom prepared for you since the creation of the world.** *For I was hungry and you gave me something to eat, I was thirsty and you gave me something to drink, I was a stranger and you invited me in.*" (Matthew 25:34,35)

I tell you the truth, *anyone who gives you a cup of water in my name because you belong to Christ* **will certainly not lose his reward.** (Mark 9:41)

The man who plants and the man who waters have one purpose, **and each will be rewarded according to his own labor.** (1 Corinthians 3:8)

My dear brothers, stand firm. Let nothing move you. *Always give yourselves fully to the work of the Lord,* **because you**

know that your labor in the Lord is not in vain.
(1 Corinthians 15:58)

Serve wholeheartedly, as if you were serving the Lord, not men, **because you know that the Lord will reward everyone for whatever good he does,** whether he is slave or free. (Ephesians 6:7,8)

Slaves, obey your earthly masters in everything; and do it, not only when their eye is on you and to win their favor, but with sincerity of heart and reverence for the Lord. *Whatever you do, work at it with all your heart, as working for the Lord, not for men,* **since you know that you will receive an inheritance from the Lord as a reward.** (Colossians 3:22-24)

Physical training is of some value, *but godliness has value for all things,* **holding promise for both the present life and the life to come.** (1 Timothy 4:8)

Command them to do good, to be rich in good deeds, and to be generous and willing to share. **In this way they will lay up treasure for themselves as a firm foundation for the coming age, so that they may take hold of the life that is truly life.** (1 Timothy 6:18)

The nations were angry; and your wrath has come. The time has come for judging the dead, *and for rewarding your servants the prophets and your saints and those who reverence your name,* both small and great. (Revelation 11:18)

Finally, note one passage from the Old Testament: Psalm 26. This and similar passages are often interpreted as if righteousness were the righteousness Christ gave us as a gift, which is imputed to us by faith. In other words, because we have faith in Jesus, God is actually looking at his Son's work and then viewing us as if we had done these works ourselves. God certainly deals with us like that. But sections of Scripture such as Psalm 26 can hardly be interpreted like that. It is clear that David is looking at what he has done in his life as a fruit of his love for God and asking that God vindicate his righteous way of living in the face of the slander of his enemies.

Vindicate me, O LORD, for I have led a blameless life;
I have trusted in the LORD without wavering.

> Test me, O LORD, and try me, examine my heart
> and my mind;
> for your love is ever before me, and I walk continually
> in your truth.
> I do not sit with deceitful men, nor do I consort
> with hypocrites;
> I abhor the assembly of evildoers and refuse to sit
> with the wicked.
> I wash my hands in innocence, and go about your altar,
> O LORD,
> proclaiming aloud your praise and telling of
> all your wonderful deeds.
> I love the house where you live, O LORD,
> the place where your glory dwells.
> Do not take away my soul along with sinners,
> my life with bloodthirsty men,
> in whose hands are wicked schemes,
> whose right hands are full of bribes.
> But I lead a blameless life; redeem me and
> be merciful to me.
> My feet stand on level ground; in the great assembly
> I will praise the LORD. (Psalm 26)

David knew he was forgiven by Christ, and he knew that his Savior's righteousness was his through faith. But he also knew that through faith he was a new creation, and as such he was willing and able to serve the Lord. According to his new man, he was a righteous person. His blameless life flowed from faith. Like Job, he would not deny the righteous life God had worked in his heart through the gospel. As happens in many other places in Scripture, David's life is spoken of as the reason why God blesses him. Can each of us Christians say the same things? Yes, we can, for Christ has forgiven us, made us new creations, and set us on the path of service to him.

These passages are not to make us proud or ambitious. Rather, they are to comfort us on our journey to eternal life. They are a part of the gospel. It is good news that the Lord will reward our labor and our struggles, if not in this life, then in the next. We stand before the Lord as people whom he has enabled to produce fruits of faith. The fruits of our faith will differ, some doing more, some doing less (Matthew 13:23). But all of us can look forward to our eternal reward and find encouragement to keep our eyes focused on the cross, where we have been renewed in the image of God.

7

The Gospel of the Kingdom

The gospel of the kingdom is closely tied together with Jewish history. If you had asked a child of Jesus' day what he hoped would happen in his lifetime, he would have said, "I want the kingdom to be restored to Israel."

The child's hope would have pleased God. God had promised Israel this would happen. The child's wish was a statement of faith in the gospel.

We won't spend a lot of time in the Old Testament explaining the history of this hope. But a few notes will help us understand what every Jewish believer was looking forward to. This, in turn, will help us see how we are involved in the fulfillment of this hope.

Ever since the people of Israel left Egypt, they were harassed by one foreign nation after another. Most of Israel's problems were its own fault. They stemmed from Israel's rebellion against God. For some three hundred years after the Israelites entered the Promised Land, God had to chasten them for worshiping the idols of the nations around them.

In time, the Israelites asked God for a king. They wanted a leader they could see and rally around, someone who would lead them into battle. God's care was not good enough for them, nor were his battle plans to their liking. After letting the people know that in asking for a king, Israel was rejecting him, God agreed.

Life under Israel's kings did not really improve Israel's win-loss rate against foreign invaders. Because Israel continued to serve idols, the Lord continued to leave its boundaries open to foreign invaders. Israel continued to be oppressed by neighboring powers. This continued until Jesus' time, when the foreign oppressor was Rome.

Yet during one very special period, Israel experienced a remarkable time of godliness and growth. This was under the second king of Israel, David. David was a God-fearing man, and the Lord blessed Israel under his rule. Israel's boundaries were extended as far as they ever would be. Under David, the Lord completely fulfilled his promise to Abraham to give his descendants all the land from Egypt north to the Euphrates River. It was a wonderful time for Israel. It lived in peace. Its king was concerned not only for its physical needs but for its spiritual needs as well. These blessings continued into the early years of the reign of David's son Solomon. Solomon too served the Lord and gave Israel strong spiritual leadership, particularly through his completion of the Lord's temple in Jerusalem.

This period of peace and prosperity was brief. But it gave Israel a glimpse into the future, to the time of an even greater kingdom. David and his kingdom served as a reference point, something the Israelites could relate to when they were told to look into the future to another time of peace and prosperity. From the time of David until God's kingdom was finally ushered in, God's prophets pointed the people ahead to this perfect kingdom. What Israel could not obtain because of its sins, the Lord himself would establish in his undeserved love. The prophet told the people that a king would come from David's line. Typical of all the prophecies of that day, Isaiah said:

> For to us a child is born, to us a son is given, and the government will be on his shoulders. And he will be called Wonderful Counselor, Mighty God, Everlasting Father, Prince of Peace. Of the increase of his government and peace there will be no end. **He will reign on David's throne and over his kingdom,** establishing and upholding it with justice and righteousness from that time on and forever. The zeal of the LORD Almighty will accomplish this. (Isaiah 9:6,7)

A kingdom with unlimited boundaries. A kingdom that would never end. A king who was none other than God himself. This the Lord would bring about by his own zeal.

The people waited. Most looked forward to a kingdom. But it was not clear to them what the kingdom would be like. Many, probably most, viewed this kingdom only in physical terms. They wanted someone to free them from the Persians, then the Greeks, and finally the Romans. They expected someone to lead Israel in battle, give it power to defeat its enemies, and then establish Jewish rule throughout the world. That's what the Jews saw in Jesus when he fed the hungry and healed the sick. That's what puzzled them when Jesus spoke about humility, love, and his own death on the cross. That's what they saw in Jesus when he entered Jerusalem on Palm Sunday. That's what destroyed their expectations when they saw him die on a cross five days later.

Yet some in Israel saw the situation clearly. When Zechariah (the father of John the Baptist, who was to announce that the King had arrived), thought ahead to Jesus, he defined Jesus' kingship like this:

> [God] has raised up a horn of salvation for us in the house of his servant David (as he said through his holy prophets of long ago), salvation from our enemies and from the hand of all who hate us—to show mercy to our fathers and to remember his holy covenant, the oath he swore to our father Abraham: to rescue us from the hand of our enemies, and to enable us to serve him without fear in holiness and righteousness before him all our days. (Luke 1:69-75)

Zechariah realized how his son, John, would prepare the people to receive this King. He would give God's people "the knowledge of salvation through the forgiveness of their sins" (Luke 1:77). Salvation would not come through armies but through the forgiveness of sins. The kingdom itself would be built around Jesus' forgiveness, and because of that it would be radically different from a kingdom built by the weapons of human warfare. People like Zechariah, John, and others realized the true nature of Jesus' kingdom. They understood how that kingdom would be established and how it would spread.

For three years Jesus worked to encourage and nurture those who understood the true nature of the kingdom he came to establish. He rebuked those who misunderstood the prophets and tried to enlighten them. He wanted them to see him for the King he was. He wanted them to become members of his kingdom. That is why John the Baptist's work was so important. He gave the people a head start on understanding Jesus. Otherwise, Jesus would have had to start from scratch and testify about himself. Matthew starts his account of John the Baptist by saying, "In those days John the Baptist came, preaching in the Desert of Judea and saying, 'Repent, for the kingdom of heaven is near'" (Matthew 3:1,2).

The word *near,* as the NIV translates it, can be misleading. The KJV translates the Greek word "at hand." *Near* implies that something is close but has not arrived. "At hand" states that something has arrived. That is what John was sent to do. John wanted to tell his people that the kingdom of God, for which they had been waiting many years, had now arrived. The King was here.

Yet confusion and controversy reigned. In some ways Jesus looked like a budding earthly king. In other ways he seemed to be the opposite. Even John the Baptist, who was chosen by God to herald the King's coming, was confused. "By now," he thought, "I should be feasting with the King, sharing his power, and making decisions on his behalf." But within a few short months after announcing the arrival of the King, he found himself rotting in the prison of another king, a wicked king named Herod, whose whole life was opposed to God.

John was apparently so troubled at Jesus' apparent lack of success that he sent some of his own disciples to Jesus with the question, "Are you the one who was to come, or should we expect someone else?" (Matthew 11:3). Jesus pointed to what he was doing—things the prophets said the coming King would do—and said:

> Go back and report to John what you hear and see: The blind receive sight, the lame walk, those who have leprosy are cured, the deaf hear, the dead are raised, and the good news is preached to the poor. Blessed is the man who does not fall away on account of me. (Matthew 11:4-6)

Blessed is the person, Jesus was saying, who does not expect a different sort of king than me, miss my kingship, and lose the kingdom of God. No, the kingdom of God has arrived.

Jesus' miracles proved that the kingdom of God was at hand. When he sent out his disciples to preach and teach in the towns and villages, he told them, "As you go, preach this message: 'The kingdom of heaven is near [at hand].' Heal the sick, raise the dead, cleanse those who have leprosy, drive out demons" (Matthew 10:7,8). When the disciples returned from their preaching tour, they were amazed that the demons were subject to them. Jesus rejoiced over their work but put things into perspective by reminding them, "However, do not rejoice that the spirits submit to you, but rejoice that your names are written in heaven" (Luke 10:20).

Once when Jesus was driving out demons, the Pharisees accused him of driving out demons by Satan's power. He said, "If I drive out demons by the Spirit of God, then the kingdom of God has come upon you" (Matthew 12:28).

Often we point to Jesus' miracles as proof that he is the Son of God. The miracles certainly prove that. But Jesus also performed miracles to demonstrate that the kingdom long awaited in Israel had come. The time of waiting was over. The Son of God had arrived with the power and compassion to heal, to calm storms, to feed masses of people, to raise the dead, and to cast out demons. Jesus' miracles were mighty acts to some people, but to a Jewish believer waiting for the Messiah and his kingdom, the miracles were proof that the

Messiah had arrived and the kingdom would once again belong to God's people. Miracles were kingdom events.

So were Jesus' words. Consider Jesus' parables. The parables were more than "earthly stories with heavenly meanings." To the disciples, who would spearhead the advance of the kingdom after Jesus returned to heaven, the parables were (or would soon become) their instruction manual on how the kingdom operated. They revealed what the disciples could expect as workers in the kingdom.

The kingdom is like a sower who has various results when he sows the seed. The disciples would find the same results when they sowed the seed of the Word. Face this reality, Jesus said. The kingdom of heaven is like seed that falls where it may, and you have no power over what happens to it after it is sown. But you can be sure that some of it will fall on rich ground and that it will grow. The kingdom is like a treasure in a field. Don't be so concerned about convincing people of the value of your message, Jesus taught his disciples. People will give up everything they have to obtain the treasure you hold out to them. The kingdom of God is like a man who sows seed in his field. Then, as he sits back and watches it grow, he has no idea how it is growing. He even sleeps, and do you know what? It still grows. Yes, the disciples could sleep in peace amidst the rigors of kingdom work.

By these parables the Lord taught the disciples and us what working in the kingdom is like. But even more to the point of what we are saying in this chapter is that the parables teach us that God's kingdom has indeed come. The disciples would soon carry on their master's work of causing the kingdom to grow.

The teaching about God's kingdom is a large subject. For our present purposes, it is enough to say that when God's kingdom came, God's people knew they had eternal protection from their enemies; they had everything they needed for their bodies and souls; they had God's blessing on every aspect of their lives; and they had a future secure in the knowledge that God was always with them. They knew that Satan could never harm them. In this kingdom they found every reason to serve the Lord.

True, there is very much a future aspect to God's kingdom, and the New Testament often refers to the glory of God's eternal kingdom. But when Jesus arrived, the kingdom arrived with him. Everything he did and said was based on his coming victory over Satan, which he would win through his death on the cross and seal with his resurrection. Every good thing belonged to the disciples right then and would be theirs forever.

One of the most difficult things for early Jewish Christians to absorb was that God's kingdom was open to Gentiles as well as Jews. The political understanding of the kingdom precluded this. After all, if the Jews were to rule the world, who would they rule except the Gentiles? It took some time before the church realized that what set Jew apart from Gentile, namely, God's Old Testament law, had been done away with in Christ and that both Jews and Gentiles could be part of a nonpolitical kingdom, a kingdom in which believers were joined with Christ, ruling over the kingdom of Satan in whatever way his kingdom tried to exert its power over them. At a council in Jerusalem some years after Jesus ascended into heaven, the church used a pointed kingdom prophecy to clarify its position. The church must not make it difficult for the Gentiles to become part of Christ's kingdom, as it was prophesied by Amos in the Old Testament:

> After this I will return and rebuild David's fallen tent. Its ruins I will rebuild, and I will restore it, that the remnant of men may seek the Lord, and all the Gentiles who bear my name, says the Lord. (Acts 15:16,17, quoting Amos 9:11,12)

So what does this all mean? It means that Jesus' kingdom was not the political kingdom many of the Jews expected. And a good thing it wasn't. A political kingdom would have helped only a part of the people of the world—the Jews. It would have excluded the Gentiles. A political kingdom would have solved only some of the people's problems—earthly problems. It would have given them freedom from oppression, a good standard of living, health, and hope for a future on earth. But a political kingdom would never have solved eternal problems, the problem of sin and our need for peace with God.

The good news is that Jesus established a kingdom that was perfect and complete. In his kingdom the thing that separated Jews and Gentiles, the law, was fulfilled and became obsolete. The kingdom was open to all people. Oppression had come to an end. In heaven the enemies of God's people are shut out from the city where God's people live. His kingdom provides freedom from the worst oppressor, the devil, whose weapons have led people into the grip of sin and hell. Through Jesus' victory on the cross, where the law was nullified, where guilt was removed, and where the forgiveness of sins was ushered in, we have access to God's love and grace. Jesus established a kingdom that gives us a place where all our physical needs will finally be met, namely, a new heaven and earth.

With this in mind, we can return to our topic of gospel motivation. The message of the kingdom helps us understand all Jesus' teachings. Everything he taught and did was set in the context of the kingdom. The kingdom of God, properly understood, is a huge, overarching concept that includes every possible blessing God wants to give us. It includes justification by faith, the gift of Christ's righteousness, God's care and guidance, and the church's victory over its enemies. It includes weapons to fight off Satan's attacks and the promise of ultimate dominion over his empire. It includes God's power to turn every hardship into victory, every need into a tool for greater growth in faith, and every joy into a reason to praise God. It provides the way we can pass through God's judgment and into his eternal kingdom.

Keeping these truths in mind, let's consider the Sermon on the Mount. The Sermon on the Mount has been used in various ways. Often it is used as a catalog of laws that Christians are to keep. At worst it is interpreted as the method Jesus gave us to find salvation. At best it is viewed as an example of the third use of the law, namely, to help believers know what to do in their lives of faith.

When it is viewed in the context of the kingdom, though, we find it no different than Paul's sermons, in which he weaves the gospel into his every admonition and encouragement. Everything Jesus tells us to do in this sermon is infused with gospel motivation.

Consider the beginning of the Sermon on the Mount. The eight Beatitudes contain encouragement for Jesus' disciples, who live with an entirely different outlook and spirit than the world. Because of this, the world looks down on them and persecutes them. The Lord comforts his people by telling them about the Lord's great blessing on their faith. Six of the Beatitudes contain promises of what the Lord will give his people. Two of them, however, tell us what the Lord is giving us right now. Those are the first and the last, which tell us that as God's people the kingdom is ours. It is a striking way of organizing the Beatitudes. It is almost as if Jesus bracketed all of God's rewards with the most all-encompassing one, the kingdom, which is a present reality and possession of those who serve the Lord.

Those who listened to the sermon (and we who read it today) were hearing everything Jesus said in light of the gospel. "You are the salt of the earth. . . . You are the light of the world" (Matthew 5:13,14). That's Jesus' way of saying that we are new creatures. If we let our salt become flat or hide our lights under a bushel basket, we are shutting Christ out of our hearts and giving up our place in the kingdom.

You are members of my kingdom, Jesus says, so things will be different for you than for those who are not in my kingdom. You are serving the one who has fulfilled every command and every prophecy ever uttered. In my kingdom you are already considered righteous and holy. For this reason, you don't have to curtail the scope of God's law as your religious leaders are doing by paring it down to size so that it fits your ability to keep it. No, those who are great in my kingdom—who really understand what it means to be a member of it and who put this into practice—teach others to do everything God wills. Why? Because where there might be failure, there is always forgiveness. And where there is obedience, it is done by God's power in Christ and to his glory. Your righteousness must be greater than the piecemeal, external righteousness of the Pharisees and teachers of the law. It must be whole and complete (and as the light and salt of the world, it will be), otherwise your end will be like theirs.

After this, Jesus compares and contrasts the righteousness of those in the kingdom with those outside of the kingdom.

Murder, anger, slander, the proper spirit of making an offering, adultery, divorce, swearing, sin in one's life, taking oaths, revenge, lawsuits, unreasonable imposition, and love for enemies are all topics Jesus wants his people to view in light of their citizenship in heaven. His people don't have to cut out of the law what they can't do, for they live under forgiving grace. We want to serve our King with all our heart, soul, and mind. We can love our enemies because our King can replace anything our enemies might unjustly take from us. For this same reason, we don't have to drag people into court. We don't have to gain satisfaction with anger, cursing, or hatred. God wants our enemies also to become part of his kingdom, and we may be the instruments he uses. We don't have to struggle to get out of an oppressive marriage, for our King is our solace and comfort. We don't have to back up our promises with oaths, since we know that as part of God's kingdom, we will be truthful like our King. You see the point. We are motivated to read and observe Jesus' instruction in the Sermon on the Mount because we are in a special kingdom ruled over by a special King. It is a rule that those outside the kingdom can't even imagine.

We can do our works of piety in secret, since we are looking for our King's approval and don't have to scramble for approval of the people of this world. We can pray with simplicity because a simple prayer is all that a gracious God asks for. We pray for spiritual blessings almost exclusively, since we know that as we do this, our King will provide everything else we need in life. Because our King has not judged, we do not judge others. We deal patiently with the faults of others, just as our King has dealt patiently with us. We pray with confidence because our King is our provider. We enter through the narrow gate of repentance and faith in the King who died for us, and we seek to serve him. We avoid the wide gate of self-righteousness and all the legal nitpicking that accompanies it.

Jesus' teaching astounded the crowds, not because he was so profound but because he spoke as someone who knew the power of the gospel of the kingdom and could speak to his subjects as objects of his grace and forgiveness.

When you read Jesus' words in the Sermon on the Mount, cover it with the gospel of the kingdom and you will find all the motivation you need to keep Jesus' words. You will also learn how the gospel of the kingdom infuses every aspect of our lives. Here is wisdom stemming from the love and power of our King.

We might say the same thing about the book of James. James does not have a lot of overt gospel motivation. But it is set in the same context as the Sermon on the Mount. James wrote to a similar audience, namely, Jewish people who had come to believe that Jesus had established God's kingdom but now needed encouragement to continue serving the Lord.

Let's finish this chapter with a few of Saint Paul's references to the kingdom. Paul did not use this concept as much as he used other concepts, perhaps because he was speaking mostly to Gentiles. The kingdom is primarily a Jewish concept. Nevertheless, as a Jew himself, Paul saw his message in kingdom terms. In fact, his entire message could be summarized as the gospel of the kingdom. The last thing Luke wrote about Paul was this:

> For two whole years Paul stayed there in his own rented house and welcomed all who came to see him. Boldly and without hindrance he preached the kingdom of God and taught about the Lord Jesus Christ. (Acts 28:30,31)

Paul refers to the kingdom of God about eight times in his letters. Sometimes he refers to the heavenly kingdom we will someday inherit. But sometimes he reminds us that we are living in the kingdom of God.

Paul uses the term in a very striking way when he speaks about "strong" Christians dealing with "weak" Christians. Strong Christians are those who can apply the freedom they have in Christ in choosing how they want to serve the Lord. Weak Christians are those who feel conscience-bound to worship God using some particular custom, perhaps one they learned when they were younger, and they can't shake themselves loose from thinking that their way is the only right way to serve. Paul addresses the strong Christian and says:

> The kingdom of God is not a matter of eating and drinking, but of righteousness, peace and joy in the Holy Spirit,

because anyone who serves Christ in this way is pleasing to
God and approved by men. (Romans 14:17,18)

Should we bicker about this custom or that custom? Should
we force people into our mode because technically we are right
and they are wrongly bound by customs God does not demand
that we use? No. The most important thing is service to Christ
that flows from hearts in which the Spirit is working.
Although the kingdom is God's rule over us, there is almost a
spatial element to the kingdom, a "place" where we are living
with fellow believers. In this place, it does not matter what we
eat or what we drink but whether we are walking righteously
before the Lord; it's a matter of resting in the peace we have
in Christ's forgiveness and being filled with joy through the
Holy Spirit because we are children of God. Paul knows that
when we remember what this kingdom is like, we will shape
our lives around it.

In Colossians 1 Paul encourages us to live lives worthy of
the Lord, to please him, to bear fruit, to grow in knowing
Christ, and to give thanks to God in a spirit of joy. He does
not just tell us to do these things, but he also reminds us
about what God has done for us. Notice how he calls the
kingdom of God the kingdom of light, in contrast to the kingdom of darkness, Satan's kingdom, out of which we have
been rescued. God has filled this new kingdom with his blessings. There we live with his Son, whom he loves. There we
are bought back from sin and death through the forgiveness
of sins.

We pray this in order that you may *live a life worthy of the
Lord and may please him in every way: bearing fruit in every
good work, growing in the knowledge of God, being strengthened with all power according to his glorious might so that
you may have great endurance and patience, and joyfully
giving thanks to the Father,* **who has qualified you to
share in the inheritance of the saints in the kingdom
of light. For he has rescued us from the dominion of
darkness and brought us into the kingdom of the Son
he loves, in whom we have redemption, the forgiveness of sins.** (Colossians 1:10-14)

What we do for God is woven together with the gospel of what he has done for us in bringing us into his kingdom.

In his first letter, Peter uses a similar picture. He calls us a people belonging to God. We are chosen; we are royalty; we are a holy nation. Each of these terms describes what it means to be members of God's kingdom.

> **You are a chosen people, a royal priesthood, a holy nation, a people belonging to God,** *that you may declare the praises of him* **who called you out of darkness into his wonderful light. Once you were not a people, but now you are the people of God; once you had not received mercy, but now you have received mercy.** *Dear friends, I urge you,* **as aliens and strangers in the world,** *to abstain from sinful desires, which war against your soul.* (1 Peter 2:9-11)

Notice the gospel concepts heaped one on top of the other. They lead us to praise the Lord and abstain from sinning while we live in this world.

Luther had it right when he said in the Small Catechism: "All this he did that I should be his own, and live under him in his kingdom, and serve him in everlasting righteousness, innocence, and blessedness." And we think of his famous hymn "A Mighty Fortress." In the fourth stanza, he wrote, "And take they our life, goods, fame, child, and wife, let these all be gone, they yet have nothing won; the Kingdom ours remaineth" (*The Lutheran Hymnal* 262:4).

8

The Gospel in the Sacraments; The Gospel of Light

The gospel in Baptism

The New Testament writers sometimes remind us that the sacraments, particularly Baptism, are great gifts to us from God.

We have already looked at one of the most important instances of how Baptism encourages us in our lives of sanctification. Paul began his discourse on our new life in Christ (Romans 6:1–8:17) by reminding us of the first event in our lives as Christians. When we were baptized, we joined Christ in his death. Through Baptism we took part in his resurrection and in the new life he lives in service to his heavenly

Father. And from that point, Paul launched into his great section on the new life we enjoy in Christ and the obligation we have to live as new creations.

When Paul wanted to encourage the Ephesian Christians to live in harmony with one another, he reminded them of everything they shared as God's people. He said:

> *Make every effort to keep the unity of the Spirit through the bond of peace.* **There is one body and one Spirit—just as you were called to one hope when you were called—one Lord, one faith, one baptism; one God and Father of all, who is over all and through all and in all.** (Ephesians 4:3-6)

We are all one in the body of Christ. We all share one Spirit. We have a single hope. We worship one Lord. We have one faith. We live under the same God who is over all people and who gives life and direction to all his creatures. We also share one Baptism. We all felt the same water poured on us, experienced the same forgiveness of sins, and heard the same message: you are baptized into the life-giving name of the Father, Son, and Holy Spirit. These reminders of what we have in common with our fellow Christians have the power to create harmony and peace among us.

Paul uses the power of our baptism in a related but somewhat different way in Colossians 2:8-14. Evidently the Colossians were having a problem understanding who Jesus was. They did not realize the full extent of his power, glory, and divine nature. The lower the value someone places on Jesus, the higher the value that person must place on his own reason and human spiritual impulses. The Colossians were substituting human customs and philosophies for Jesus.

Paul told the Colossians that "all the fullness of the Deity" lives in Christ in bodily form. And we have been given fullness in Christ. Jesus rules over every power and authority, physical and spiritual, in this age. What's more, through his power our hearts have been circumcised and cut free from sin. How? Through our baptism and union with Christ in his death and resurrection. This is an abbreviated presentation of what Paul explained in Romans 6 and 7. Here is what Paul wrote to the Colossians:

> *See to it that no one takes you captive through hollow and deceptive philosophy,* which depends on human tradition and the basic principles of this world rather than on Christ. **For in Christ all the fullness of the Deity lives in bodily form, and you have been given fullness in Christ, who is the head over every power and authority. In him you were also circumcised, in the putting off of the sinful nature, not with a circumcision done by the hands of men but with the circumcision done by Christ, having been buried with him in baptism and raised with him through your faith in the power of God, who raised him from the dead. When you were dead in your sins and in the uncircumcision of your sinful nature, God made you alive with Christ. He forgave us all our sins, having canceled the written code, with its regulations, that was against us and that stood opposed to us; he took it away, nailing it to the cross.** (Colossians 2:8-14)

Paul could simply have told the Colossians to put away their human ceremonies and philosophies and believe in Jesus. But he goes further. He unfolds to us what it means to have Jesus. We experience the power of the gospel cutting off our sinful natures every day. And that is something that no human philosophy or system of religion based on the "basic principles of this world" could ever do. Nor could these philosophies put the law to death. Nor could they give us the fullness of all the blessings God pours out on us in Christ, who contains in himself as the God-man the fullness of God himself. Many thoughts are all woven together into a beautiful picture of what we have in Christ, motivating us to give up the ways and means of the world—and what is the connecting link between Christ and us? Baptism.

In addition to temptations to follow worldly wisdom and philosophy, we face temptations to give up faith to avoid persecution. That's one of the main reasons Peter wrote his first letter to the congregations Paul had started in Galatia. He encouraged them:

> It is better, if it is God's will, to suffer for doing good than for doing evil. . . . **Therefore, since Christ suffered in his body,** *arm yourselves also with the same attitude,* because he who has suffered in his body is done with sin. As a result, he does not live the rest of his earthly life for evil human desires, but rather for the will of God. (1 Peter 3:17; 4:1,2)

Peter could simply have told his readers to "buck up" and take the persecution that came their way. But that would have accomplished nothing. Between 3:17 and 4:1,2 (where Peter encouraged his readers), Peter sandwiches a beautiful section of gospel:

> Christ died for sins once for all, the righteous for the unrighteous, to bring you to God. He was put to death in the body but made alive by the Spirit, through whom also he went and preached to the spirits in prison who disobeyed long ago when God waited patiently in the days of Noah while the ark was being built. In it only a few people, eight in all, were saved through water, and this water symbolizes baptism that now saves you also—not the removal of dirt from the body but the pledge of a good conscience toward God. It saves you by the resurrection of Jesus Christ, who has gone into heaven and is at God's right hand—with angels, authorities and powers in submission to him. (1 Peter 3:18-22)

What is the link between Jesus' suffering and our resurrection? Baptism. Baptism buoys us up above the destruction coming on the world. How? By uniting us with Jesus' resurrection and giving us a clean conscience. This hope, given us by our baptism, will carry us through any suffering we are called on to endure.

We might also mention Titus 3:4-7. These words contain many clear and beautiful statements about our faith. They include a fine description of what God did for us at our baptism: "He saved us through the washing of rebirth." That is a washing which led to a rebirth into God's family and salvation from sin and its results. Paul writes:

> **When the kindness and love of God our Savior appeared, he saved us, not because of righteous things we had done, but because of his mercy. He**

saved us through the washing of rebirth and renewal by the Holy Spirit, whom he poured out on us generously through Jesus Christ our Savior, so that, having been justified by his grace, we might become heirs having the hope of eternal life. (Titus 3:4-7)

Just like the passage from 1 Peter above, this passage is sandwiched between encouragements to serve the Lord. At the beginning of chapter 3, Paul told Titus:

Remind the people *to be subject to rulers and authorities, to be obedient, to be ready to do whatever is good, to slander no one, to be peaceable and considerate, and to show true humility toward all men.* (Titus 3:1,2)

Right after the gospel section quoted above, Paul wrote:

This is a trustworthy saying. And I want you to stress these things, *so that those who have trusted in God may be careful to devote themselves to doing what is good.* (Titus 3:8)

Encouragement to live a godly life, followed by the gospel, followed by more encouragement—that's the pattern. And remember, the writers are not using the gospel to motivate people. They are stressing the importance of godly living on the part of those who have the gospel. The gospel motivates only because it is the heart of a Christian's life.

The gospel in the Lord's Supper

On the night Jesus was betrayed, he gave his disciples the Lord's Supper. In that Supper he gave them to eat and to drink his body and blood for the forgiveness of their sins. It was to be a meal shared by his disciples on a regular basis until he came again. It was a meal by which they would remember all he had done for them.

The New Testament writers do not refer to the Lord's Supper very often. It is, rather, in the background, something the church continues to do. On one occasion, however, Paul used the Lord's Supper to lead one of his congregations, the Corinthians, to change its way of acting.

The congregation Paul started in Corinth had its share of problems. One of its problems was disharmony in worship

services. In 1 Corinthians 11, Paul criticized the members of
the congregation for how they treated one another. In the fellowship meal after the service, when they ate and drank the
Lord's Supper, they were treating one another almost as enemies. The rich would dive into their lavish meals and make
the poor wait over in the corner until they were done eating.
Freemen looked down on slaves as second-class citizens.
Then they would celebrate the Lord's Supper together, confess their sins, and receive God's forgiveness. What a joke!
Perhaps the rich even thought they were richer in God's
mercy than the poor.

How did Paul solve the problem? Since the problem centered on how they celebrated the Lord's Supper, why not bring
out the gospel beauty in the Lord's Supper? That's what Paul
did. He repeated the words of institution of the Lord's Supper,
which the Lord Jesus had given him by revelation:

> I received from the Lord what I also passed on to you: The
> Lord Jesus, on the night he was betrayed, took bread, and
> when he had given thanks, he broke it and said, "This is my
> body, which is for you; do this in remembrance of me." In the
> same way, after supper he took the cup, saying, "This cup is
> the new covenant in my blood; do this, whenever you drink
> it, in remembrance of me." For whenever you eat this bread
> and drink this cup, you proclaim the Lord's death until he
> comes. (1 Corinthians 11:23-26)

Jesus is saying, "This is my body. I gave it for you. This cup
is the new covenant of mercy and forgiveness. When you drink
it, remember me. I have saved you all from your sins. When
you gather together in my name and celebrate the Lord's Supper, you, my people, are proclaiming that you are all sinners
and that my death has redeemed you all, small and great.
Someday I will come again, and I want to find you still cele-
brating my Supper."

Paul then gave the Corinthians some very stern words in
the verses that follow. They should be afraid of God's judgment in view of how they were treating their fellow believers
and how they were denying their need for Jesus' body and
blood even as they were eating and drinking it. But when they

took Paul's warnings to heart, they could look back on his description of the Lord's Supper and shape their lives around it. They would remember that Christ died for their sins and that they were no less sinners than the poor people in their congregation. They would look at one another not as rivals but as brothers and sisters in Christ. They would eat and drink the Lord's Supper in a spirit of humility, and that humility would enable them to deal with others in a God-pleasing way. When we see our fellow brothers and sisters in Christ going to the Lord's Supper and we join them there, hostility, jealousy, snobbery, and a host of other evils melt away. We see them as fellow travelers with us on the road to eternal life, waiting for Jesus to come again.

The gospel of light

The contrast between light and darkness is one of the most vivid and often-used pictures in Scripture. It is gospel, and the Bible writers use it to remind us of what we have in Christ. It is so simple that a young child can understand it. Go into a dark room and flip on the switch. Not knowing what's in the room, not being able to walk around in it without stumbling, facing the possibility that someone or something evil is lurking there—this is all replaced by a clear understanding of what is there, the ability to walk where you want and defend yourself if necessary. Anyone can understand this picture.

It's a powerful picture to describe one's relation to God and the devil, to goodness and evil, to salvation and punishment. Darkness is not knowing God and, even worse, not realizing that you are living for Satan. Darkness is confusion over goodness and evil; it is not really understanding that true goodness can only be inspired by God's grace. Darkness is looking at death with a big question mark or, more honestly, in complete fear. Light is the opposite. A person who stands in the light of Jesus and his revelation of God the Father knows God, flees the devil, loves good, hates evil. He knows that he can face death, for in Christ he has already died and risen again, and that his death is but a continuation of the life he has now, but far greater.

Without Christ we were in the darkness. With him we are in the light. Matthew quoted Isaiah, who foretold Jesus' coming to his people and what would happen when he appeared:

> The people living in darkness have seen a great light; on those living in the land of the shadow of death a light has dawned. (Matthew 4:16 quoting Isaiah 9:2)

The faithful believer Simeon saw the baby Jesus in the temple and said of him:

> My eyes have seen your salvation, which you have prepared in the sight of all people, a light for revelation to the Gentiles and for glory to your people Israel. (Luke 2:30-32)

The gospel writer John also spoke in terms of light versus darkness:

> In [Jesus] was life, and that life was the light of men. The light shines in the darkness, but the darkness has not understood it. There came a man who was sent from God; his name was John. He came as a witness to testify concerning that light, so that through him all men might believe. He himself was not the light; he came only as a witness to the light. The true light that gives light to every man was coming into the world. (John 1:4-9)

At some time in your life, you have probably turned over a rock or a piece of wood that has been lying out in the rain for a long time. You picked it up and discovered a whole subculture of bugs and worms that had made that place of darkness their home. As soon as the light strikes these creatures, they scurry around trying to find darkness. They cannot tolerate the light. You have also seen a plant growing out of the soil. From the first moment it poked its head out of the soil, it has lived on light. It needs light to grow. If you turn the plant around so its leaves are facing away from the light, the leaves will soon turn their faces around so they are once more facing the light.

On one occasion, Jesus warned a man named Nicodemus to seek out the light, like a plant:

> This is the verdict: Light has come into the world, but men loved darkness instead of light because their deeds were

evil. Everyone who does evil hates the light, and will not come into the light for fear that his deeds will be exposed. But whoever lives by the truth comes into the light, so that it may be seen plainly that what he has done has been done through God. (John 3:19-21)

In effect, Jesus was saying, "Nicodemus, there are two kinds of people in this world. One kind of person lives in the darkness and does the deeds of darkness. He refuses to come into my light. When my light shines on him, he covers his eyes and ducks into the darkness. And tragically, darkness will be his eternal fate. The other kind of person has been born as a child of God. He is happy to come into my light, because his deeds have been inspired and motivated by God. He will live in my light into eternity. Nicodemus, be that kind of person."

On several occasions, Jesus spoke to the crowds about the light, encouraging them to come into the light.

When Jesus spoke again to the people, he said, "I am the light of the world. Whoever follows me will never walk in darkness, but will have the light of life." (John 8:12)

Then Jesus told them, "You are going to have the light just a little while longer. Walk while you have the light, before darkness overtakes you. The man who walks in the dark does not know where he is going. Put your trust in the light while you have it, so that you may become sons of light." (John 12:35,36)

I have come into the world as a light, so that no one who believes in me should stay in darkness. (John 12:46)

This picture, painted in only two colors, is worth a thousand words. By God's grace we left the darkness and came into the light. Using the two words *darkness* and *light* as a sort of shorthand, Jesus and the epistle writers flood our minds with images of the salvation we have in Jesus. They then encourage us to live as children of the light.

Paul encouraged the Ephesians just as Jesus encouraged Nicodemus:

You were once darkness, but now you are light in the Lord. *Live **as children of light** (for the fruit of the light*

> *consists in all goodness, righteousness and truth) and find
> out what pleases the Lord. Have nothing to do with the fruit-
> less deeds of darkness,* but rather expose them. For it is
> shameful even to mention what the disobedient do in secret.
> But everything exposed by the light becomes visible, for it is
> light that makes everything visible. This is why it is said:
> "Wake up, O sleeper, rise from the dead, and Christ will
> shine on you." (Ephesians 5:8-14)

The light of Christ has shined on us and has made us light. By
God's grace we are awake and alive in him. By means of that
light, we can see clearly. We understand God and his will. We
know how to serve him. We know how to expose the deeds of
darkness. "Live as those on whom the light has shined," Paul
is saying.

Paul weaves the picture of light and darkness together with
the day of Christ's second coming. The night of this present
world and its evil is soon to be taken over by the day of God's
new heaven and earth. Yet even in this dark world we live in,
the Lord has given us the armor of light—the clothing of
Jesus Christ—to ward off the darkness.

> **The night is nearly over; the day is almost here.** *So let
> us put aside the deeds of darkness and put on the armor of
> light. Let us behave decently,* **as in the daytime,** not in
> orgies and drunkenness, not in sexual immorality and
> debauchery, not in dissension and jealousy. Rather, **clothe
> yourselves with the Lord Jesus Christ,** *and do not
> think about how to gratify the desires of the sinful nature.*
> (Romans 13:12-14)

Our friends, particularly those to whom we entrust ourselves in our deepest needs and whose faith and way of life
influence our own, must be chosen carefully. Paul tells us:

> *Do not be yoked together with unbelievers.* For what do **right-
> eousness** and wickedness have in common? Or what fellow-
> ship can **light** have with darkness? (2 Corinthians 6:14)

> **You are all sons of the light and sons of the day.** We do
> not belong to the night or to the darkness. So then, let us not
> be like others, who are asleep, *but let us be alert and self-
> controlled.* For those who sleep, sleep at night, and those

who get drunk, get drunk at night. But **since we belong to the day,** *let us be self-controlled,* putting on faith and love as a breastplate, and the hope of salvation as a helmet. **For God did not appoint us to suffer wrath but to receive salvation through our Lord Jesus Christ.** (1 Thessalonians 5:5-9)

In the next passage, Paul links light and darkness with the teaching of God's kingdom. God's kingdom is the kingdom of light. Satan's kingdom is the kingdom of darkness. That's the kingdom we were members of, but we qualified to live in a different kingdom, the kingdom of the Son he loves.

> . . . *giving thanks to the Father,* **who has qualified you to share in the inheritance of the saints in the kingdom of light. For he has rescued us from the dominion of darkness and brought us into the kingdom of the Son he loves, in whom we have redemption, the forgiveness of sins.** (Colossians 1:12-14)

Give thanks—that's part of our sanctified lives. Notice how Paul encourages us. In addition to his reminder that we are in the light, he heaps one gospel concept on another. God has "qualified you," reminding us of our faith in Christ's forgiveness. He has given us an "inheritance." We are "saints." We live in "the kingdom of light," which is also the kingdom of his Son. Don't forget the little addition "he loves." Of course that refers to the Father's love for Jesus, but if we are in the kingdom of the Son he loves, then he loves us too. In him we have "redemption," and we have "the forgiveness of sins." Yes, Paul tells us to live in a spirit of thanks, but in the same stroke, he points us to the good news of what we have in Christ.

The writer to the Hebrews uses the picture of light to encourage his readers to stand firm in persecution:

> Remember those earlier days after you had received the light, when you stood your ground in a great contest in the face of suffering. (Hebrews 10:32)

Finally, Peter encourages us to abstain from sinful desires because of what we are. In his list of reasons to keep away from evil and to guard ourselves from sin, he includes the wonderful light into which Christ has welcomed us:

> **You are a chosen people, a royal priesthood, a holy nation, a people belonging to God,** *that you may declare the praises* **of him who called you out of darkness into his wonderful light. Once you were not a people, but now you are the people of God; once you had not received mercy, but now you have received mercy. Dear friends, I urge you, as aliens and strangers in the world,** *to abstain from sinful desires, which war against your soul.* (1 Peter 2:9-11)

When you wonder where your life is going, remember this simple picture. With the light shining on you and around you, you know you are not consigned to walking in darkness like so many. You may not know exactly where you are going, but you see the wrong and you can avoid it; you see your Savior, and his grace and power go with you; and in the distance you see the light of eternal life shining at the end of your path.

9

The Gospel of Eternal Life

By this time in our study, we realize that many of the themes overlap. In this chapter we will meet a few passages we have already highlighted. But here we will look at them from yet another standpoint. One of the most important reasons for serving our Lord is the inheritance awaiting us at the end of our lives.

To stray from the path and follow the narrow road that leads to destruction is to be avoided at all costs. As Jesus says in the Sermon on the Mount, "If your right eye causes you to sin, gouge it out and throw it away. It is better for you to lose one part of your body than for your whole body to be thrown into hell" (Matthew 5:29).

The apostles saw Jesus' return as being right around the corner. They saw heaven quickly approaching. Living in eternity with Jesus was a reality as vivid and concrete as going to work or eating a meal with one's family. The apostles may not have been able to answer every question about what heaven was like, but it was nothing abstract.

Paul encourages us to set aside the deeds of darkness. Why? "Because our salvation is nearer now than when we first believed," and "the day is almost here." He writes:

> Do this, understanding the present time. *The hour has come for you to wake up from your slumber,* **because our salvation is nearer now than when we first believed. The night is nearly over; the day is almost here.** *So let us put aside the deeds of darkness and put on the armor of light. Let us behave decently, as in the daytime, not in orgies and drunkenness, not in sexual immorality and debauchery, not in dissension and jealousy.* **Rather, clothe yourselves with the Lord Jesus Christ,** *and do not think about how to gratify the desires of the sinful nature.* (Romans 13:11-14)

Paul weaves the theme of eternal life into his encouragement to the Philippians. He focuses on the contrast between those who live as God's people and those who do not. Those who live apart from Christ present a frightening picture:

> *Join with others in following my example, brothers, and take note of those who live according to the pattern we gave you.* For, as I have often told you before and now say again even with tears, many live as enemies of the cross of Christ. Their destiny is destruction, their god is their stomach, and their glory is in their shame. Their mind is on earthly things. **But our citizenship is in heaven.** And we eagerly await a Savior from there, the Lord Jesus Christ, who, by the power that enables him to bring everything under his control, **will transform our lowly bodies so that they will be like his glorious body.** (Philippians 3:17-21)

Many are enemies of the cross of Christ. They have substituted their own stomachs for God and will have nothing left but destruction when their god is destroyed in death. They have substituted the glory of God for the "glory" of sin, which they will be ashamed of when they discover what sin's wages are. Consequently, all they can think about are earthly things.

But we who believe in Christ have a treasure awaiting us when Jesus brings everything under his control and changes our mortal bodies so they will be like his glorious body. This hope motivates us to imitate mature Christians like Paul.

As Paul encouraged the Philippians, he described the Christian life as one of confidence, prayer, and thanksgiving. Why? Because "the Lord is near."

> *Let your gentleness be evident to all.* **The Lord is near.** *Do not be anxious about anything,* but in everything, by prayer and petition, with thanksgiving, *present your requests to God.* **And the peace of God, which transcends all understanding, will guard your hearts and your minds in Christ Jesus.** (Philippians 4:5-7)

Approaching this from a little different slant, Paul told Timothy to "take hold of the eternal life to which you were called." Our salvation is sure in Christ, but if we do not live according to the Spirit and "pursue righteousness, godliness, faith, love, endurance and gentleness," we are in danger of losing eternal life. Paul writes:

> But you, man of God, *flee from all this, and pursue righteousness, godliness, faith, love, endurance and gentleness. Fight the good fight of the faith.* Take hold of **the eternal life to which you were called** when you made your good confession in the presence of many witnesses. In the sight of God, **who gives life to everything,** and of Christ Jesus, who while testifying before Pontius Pilate made the good confession, *I charge you to keep this command without spot or blame* **until the appearing of our Lord Jesus Christ, which God will bring about in his own time—God, the blessed and only Ruler, the King of kings and Lord of lords**. (1 Timothy 6:11-15)

Paul points ahead to Christ's second coming and reminds us of the grace God has given us. "Live in view of the grace you have received," he is saying, "until Jesus, our God and Savior, appears."

Paul encouraged Titus:

> **The grace of God that brings salvation has appeared to all men.** *It teaches us to say "No" to ungodliness and*

> *worldly passions, and to live self-controlled, upright and godly lives in this present age,* **while we wait for the blessed hope—the glorious appearing of our great God and Savior, Jesus Christ, who gave himself for us to redeem us from all wickedness and to purify for himself a people that are his very own, eager to do what is good.** (Titus 2:11-14)

The writer to the Hebrews uses the nearness of Jesus' second coming to encourage us to encourage one another. (He also proclaims God's law, that is, the judgment that will replace eternal life with God if we continue to sin.)

> Let us not give up meeting together, as some are in the habit of doing, *but let us encourage one another*—and all the more **as you see the Day approaching.** If we deliberately keep on sinning after we have received the knowledge of the truth, no sacrifice for sins is left, but only a fearful expectation of judgment and of raging fire that will consume the enemies of God. (Hebrews 10:25-27)

The writer to the Hebrews contrasts the mountain where the Israelites stood and received God's Law (Mount Sinai) with the mountain where God's people stand at the foot of the cross and at the empty tomb (Mount Zion, the new Jerusalem). The contrast displays the blessings we have in Christ. Fear has been replaced by joy. We no longer stand under God's judgment but in the heavenly Jerusalem—we are there now—in the presence of the living God. We stand in the presence of the angels along with the "church of the firstborn, whose names are written in heaven." We are one of "the spirits of righteous men made perfect" through the new covenant established on the "sprinkled blood" of Christ.

> **You have come to Mount Zion, to the heavenly Jerusalem, the city of the living God. You have come to thousands upon thousands of angels in joyful assembly, to the church of the firstborn, whose names are written in heaven. You have come to God, the judge of all men, to the spirits of righteous men made perfect, to Jesus the mediator of a new covenant, and to the sprinkled blood that speaks a better word than**

the blood of Abel. *See to it that you do not refuse him who speaks.* If they did not escape when they refused him who warned them on earth, how much less will we, if we turn away from him who warns us from heaven? At that time his voice shook the earth, but now he has promised, "Once more I will shake not only the earth but also the heavens." The words "once more" indicate the removing of what can be shaken—that is, created things—so that what cannot be shaken may remain. **Therefore, since we are receiving a kingdom that cannot be shaken,** *let us be thankful, and so worship God acceptably with reverence and awe,* for our "God is a consuming fire." (Hebrews 12:22-29)

How can we turn away from such a great salvation?

We no longer live in ignorance. We stand in the presence of God now through the promises of his Word, and later, we will be there body and soul. Peter encourages us to reject the pleasures and passions of the world. Why? Because God's gracious eternal life is coming soon.

> *Prepare your minds for action; be self-controlled;* **set your hope fully on the grace to be given you when Jesus Christ is revealed.** As **obedient children,** *do not conform to the evil desires you had when you lived in ignorance.* (1 Peter 1:13,14)

In his second letter, Peter reminds us that this world is coming to an end. It will be burned in fire, and God will create a new heaven and a new earth. This is what we are looking forward to, and on this hope Peter bases his admonition in the last verse.

> The day of the Lord will come like a thief. The heavens will disappear with a roar; the elements will be destroyed by fire, and the earth and everything in it will be laid bare. Since everything will be destroyed in this way, what kind of people ought you to be? *You ought to live holy and godly lives* **as you look forward to the day of God and speed its coming.** That day will bring about the destruction of the heavens by fire, and the elements will melt in the heat. But in keeping with his promise we are looking forward to a new heaven and a new earth, the home of righteousness. So then, *dear friends, since you are looking forward to this, make*

every effort to be found spotless, blameless and at peace with him. (2 Peter 3:10-14)

The saying goes, "Don't be so heavenly bound that you are of no earthly good." That may be true in some cases. But the hope of heaven is one of the most compelling reasons we have to "make every effort to be found spotless, blameless and at peace with him." Who can be like that and still be of no earthly good? We who have those characteristics cannot help but be the salt of the earth and the light of the world, preserving this world for another day of gospel preaching and showing the way to heaven through our witness as God gives us opportunity.

10

The Gospel of Our Fellowship
in Christ; Prayers for One Another

Our fellowship in Christ

In the third article of the Apostles' Creed, we confess, "I believe in the holy Christian church, the communion of saints." We confess that throughout the world there exists a group of people who share the same confession and faith as we. Some of those people we know well. They are in our congregation or synod. Some may not be of our denomination, but we have come to know them as brothers or sisters in Christ through our conversations with them. Regarding most of the members of the holy Christian church, however, we have no knowledge of where they are. Even if we could see them all, we would still be short of knowing them all, because most of them have already died, and many more are yet to be born.

Our fellowship with the members of God's church is an off-shoot of the gospel. We are not alone. The Spirit continues to work in the hearts of other people as he has worked in us. Our fellowship in Christ motivates us to live in a way consistent with the gospel.

Some of Paul's churches had a problem with Christians running roughshod over fellow Christians' ideas about what they could or could not do.

> If your brother is distressed because of what you eat, you are no longer acting in love. *Do not by your eating destroy your brother* **for whom Christ died.** *Do not destroy* **the work of God** for the sake of food. All food is clean, but it is wrong for a man to eat anything that causes someone else to stumble. (Romans 14:15,20)

Notice that even when Paul is rebuking his fellow Christians, he weaves in the gospel, which encourages and motivates his readers. In the previous passage, Paul appeals to the fact that Christ died for each and every one of our fellow Christians. Every Christian is the work of God.

Paul wrote to the Corinthians:

> If anyone with a weak conscience sees you who have this knowledge eating in an idol's temple, won't he be emboldened to eat what has been sacrificed to idols? So this weak brother, **for whom Christ died,** is destroyed by your knowledge. When you sin against your brothers in this way and wound their weak conscience, you sin against Christ. *Therefore, if what I eat causes my brother to fall into sin, I will never eat meat again, so that I will not cause him to fall.* (1 Corinthians 8:10-13)

This section from Corinthians deals with the same topic as the previous section from Romans 14. But here in Corinthians, Paul adds a thought to what he wrote in Romans 14 that expands his point. In verse 12 he says, "When you sin against your brothers in this way . . . you sin against Christ." This only makes sense. If Christ is living within us, if he is the head of the body, the church, if the church is the bridegroom of Christ, if we are joined with Christ in his death and resurrection and are now with him in heaven, then any sin against a brother or sister in Christ is a sin against Christ himself. This, of course, is a strong warning. But it also reminds us of what the fellowship of believers is—a group of people "in Christ," our Savior.

The teaching of Christian fellowship comes out clearly in Romans 16. The chapter begins with a list of names, associates of Paul. When we are finished reading Romans, we are tempted to race over those names. But if we read them slowly, we find evidence of Paul's profound and grateful understanding of the fellowship he has with others in Christ.

In this section we see a deep love between Paul and the people he asks the Romans to greet. Paul had never visited Rome. But he knew people from there—people he had previously worked with who had then settled in Rome. As he greeted them by name, the way he spoke about them made the readers of this book, the Romans, appreciate the close bond that exists between fellow believers. That bond, created by the gospel, would motivate them to be united around the teachings of the faith and work together to spread the kingdom of God.

I commend to you our sister Phoebe, a servant of the church in Cenchrea. *I ask you to receive her* **in the Lord** in a way worthy of the saints and to give her any help she may need from you, for she has been a great help to many people, including me. *Greet Priscilla and Aquila,* my fellow workers **in Christ Jesus.** They risked their lives for me. Not only I but all the churches of the Gentiles are grateful to them. Greet also the church that meets at their house. *Greet my dear friend Epenetus,* who was the first **convert to Christ** in the province of Asia. Greet Mary, who worked very hard for you. *Greet Andronicus and Junias,* my relatives who have been in prison with me. They are outstanding among the apostles, and they were **in Christ** before I was. *Greet Ampliatus,* whom I love **in the Lord.** *Greet Urbanus,* our fellow worker **in Christ,** *and my dear friend Stachys. Greet Apelles,* tested and approved **in Christ.** Greet those who belong to the household of Aristobulus. Greet Herodion, my relative. *Greet those in the household of Narcissus who are* **in**

> **the Lord.** *Greet Tryphena and Tryphosa,* those women who work hard **in the Lord.** *Greet my dear friend Persis,* another woman who has worked very hard **in the Lord.** *Greet Rufus,* **chosen in the Lord,** and his mother, who has been a mother to me, too. Greet Asyncritus, Phlegon, Hermes, Patrobas, Hermas and the brothers with them. *Greet Philologus, Julia, Nereus and his sister, and Olympas* and all **the saints** with them. Greet one another with a holy kiss. All the churches of Christ send greetings. (Romans 16:1-16)

Phoebe was probably the one who delivered this letter to the Romans. She was a "servant of the church in Cenchrea." The Roman church members may not have known her. Paul realized, however, that they had a bond with her much stronger than friendship. They were to receive her "in the Lord." They were to give her whatever help she needed. Paul was confident that anything she might ask of them would be within reason and necessary for the work of the kingdom. She had already been a great help to many people, including Paul.

Priscilla and Aquila were Paul's "fellow workers." In Christian love they had worked with Paul and risked their lives for him. They were workers along with Paul "in Christ Jesus." We are only three verses into this chapter and already we have heard the phrases "in the Lord" and "in Christ Jesus." If you wish, count how many more times these phrases are used in these verses. It is clear that the love Paul had for these people was grounded in their fellowship in the gospel and their common work of building the kingdom. By the time Paul wrote this letter, his friends may have become normal working members of a church in Rome. Perhaps they were being taken for granted by the natives in Rome. Perhaps they were wishing for the more adventurous times they had with Paul. Paul's continued use of the phrases "in the Lord" and "in Christ" reminded them and their fellow church members that Christian service is never to be taken for granted, nor is it to be despised if it is less than glamorous. It is done "in the Lord," and that makes it worth doing.

In a similar vein, note how Paul encouraged two women at Philippi who seemed not to be getting along with each other. He writes:

> I plead with Euodia and I plead with Syntyche *to agree with each other* **in the Lord.** Yes, and I ask you, loyal yokefellow, *help these women* who have contended at my side **in the cause of the gospel,** *along with Clement and the rest of my fellow workers,* **whose names are in the book of life.** (Philippians 4:2,3)

He reminded the two women that they are "in the Lord." He reminded them and the congregation in Philippi that these women had worked alongside Paul. Paul encouraged peace between these women. He also encouraged congregation members who may be watching them argue to nevertheless help them and not look down on them because they contended at Paul's side "in the cause of the gospel." The work that these women, along with the rest of Paul's fellow workers, were doing was valuable, for it was work done by people "whose names are in the book of life," and it was being done for others whose names are written in the same book.

The bond of fellowship was being broken by the members of the church in Corinth because they were choosing favorite teachers and forming cliques around them. Notice how Paul dealt with the problem:

> *So then, no more boasting about men!* All things are yours, whether Paul or Apollos or Cephas or the world or life or death or the present or the future—**all are yours, and you are of Christ, and Christ is of God.** (1 Corinthians 3:21-23)

Paul appealed to their unity in Christ. All these men were united in working on behalf of all the Corinthians, because they were in the body of Christ. In fact, Paul says, everything in all creation is programmed by God to serve you—you who are "of Christ" and linked with the Creator of all through him. Your fellowship in the body of Christ, Paul says, goes far beyond any disjointed fellowship you might have in a clique.

Unity in the body of Christ also guides Christians in how they use spiritual gifts. Not envy but mutual service in love is the order of the day.

> The body is a unit, though it is made up of many parts; and
> though all its parts are many, they form one body. So it is
> with Christ. For we were all baptized by one Spirit into one
> body—whether Jews or Greeks, slave or free—and we were
> all given the one Spirit to drink. (1 Corinthians 12:12,13)

Humility and patience, love and peace are to be fostered by
those in the Christian fellowship. There is one body, one
Spirit, one Lord, etc. Because "we are all members of one
body," falsehood and lies have no place in the Christian
church. Paul writes:

> Be completely humble and gentle; be patient, bearing with
> one another in love. *Make every effort to keep the unity of the
> Spirit through the bond of peace.* **There is one body and
> one Spirit—just as you were called to one hope when
> you were called—one Lord, one faith, one baptism;
> one God and Father of all, who is over all and through
> all and in all.** Therefore each of you must *put off falsehood
> and speak truthfully to his neighbor,* for we are **all mem-
> bers of one body.** (Ephesians 4:2-6,25)

Peter describes the gospel of our fellowship in Christ in
beautiful picture language. We are "chosen," "royal," a "priesthood," "holy," "belonging to God." We are united as one people
in a nation he has created for himself:

> **You are a chosen people, a royal priesthood, a holy
> nation, a people belonging to God,** *that you may declare
> the praises of him* **who called you out of darkness into
> his wonderful light. Once you were not a people, but
> now you are the people of God; once you had not
> received mercy, but now you have received mercy.**
> *Dear friends, I urge you,* **as aliens and strangers in the
> world,** *to abstain from sinful desires, which war against your
> soul.* Live such good lives among the pagans that, though
> they accuse you of doing wrong, they may see your good
> deeds and glorify God on the day he visits us. (1 Peter 2:9-12)

What impact does this have on us? We have fellowship in
Christ and with one another so that we may "declare the
praises of him who called you out of darkness into his wonderful light." We are citizens of heaven, "the people of God."

For this reason we live as strangers in this world and abstain from the sinful desires that are so much a part of this present age.

Prayers for one another

The knowledge we have of Christ, the righteousness we have in him, and our freedom from the law is the power by which we put to death the misdeeds of the body. In fact, our inheritance in heaven, our fellowship in Christ, the knowledge of the kingdom, the blessings found in the sacraments, the light we have in Christ—all these truths impel us forward through a sort of logic. It is a spiritual logic, used by the Holy Spirit to lead us to faith and convince us to live as the new creations we have become. In other words, how we live can only follow logically from what we are.

But this logic would never do anything unless the Lord was blessing us daily, leading us to greater depth of insight into the nature of the gospel and its ramifications. We know that the Holy Spirit works through the gospel and that when we read Scripture, the Spirit is working in our hearts. Yet at the same time, we pray that God would bless his gospel among us and enable us to believe it, grow in it, and serve the Lord because of it.

That's what Paul does. He prays for his congregations. To the Colossians he wrote:

> For this reason, since the day we heard about you, we have not stopped praying for you and asking God to fill you with the knowledge of his will through all spiritual wisdom and understanding. And we pray this in order that you may live a life worthy of the Lord and may please him in every way: bearing fruit in every good work, growing in the knowledge of God, being strengthened with all power according to his glorious might so that you may have great endurance and patience, and joyfully giving thanks to the Father, who has qualified you to share in the inheritance of the saints in the kingdom of light. (Colossians 1:9-12)

Read the following beautiful words Paul wrote to the Ephesians:

> For this reason, ever since I heard about your faith in the Lord Jesus and your love for all the saints, I have not stopped giving thanks for you, remembering you in my prayers. I keep asking that the God of our Lord Jesus Christ, the glorious Father, may give you the Spirit of wisdom and revelation, so that you may know him better. I pray also that the eyes of your heart may be enlightened in order that you may know the hope to which he has called you, the riches of his glorious inheritance in the saints, and his incomparably great power for us who believe. That power is like the working of his mighty strength, which he exerted in Christ when he raised him from the dead and seated him at his right hand in the heavenly realms, far above all rule and authority, power and dominion, and every title that can be given, not only in the present age but also in the one to come. And God placed all things under his feet and appointed him to be head over everything for the church, which is his body, the fullness of him who fills everything in every way. (Ephesians 1:15-23)

This is what you and I need. We need "the Spirit of wisdom and revelation" so that we "may know him better." We need the eyes of our hearts opened and enlightened to better know and understand "the hope to which he has called" us, that is, "the riches of his glorious inheritance" and "his incomparably great power for us who believe." This power, which can raise us from whatever spiritual lethargy we are caught up in, is just like the "working of his mighty strength, which he exerted in Christ when he raised him from the dead and seated him at his right hand."

This is what we need. We do not need some mystical experience that might give us power of sorts. We do not need some tragic experience to jolt us awake, although God could use that if he wished. What we need are the facts, just the facts, emblazoned on our hearts and minds. We need to clearly see where we would be headed apart from Christ and where we will be headed with him at the lead. The more we see the contrast between the darkness we were in and the light that now shines on us, the more we will say, "Wow!" and the more we will dedicate our lives to the One who has done such great things for us. That is what Paul prays will happen to us through God's grace and power. That is what we, as members of the fellowship of Christ, should pray on behalf of our fellow Christians.

Paul prayed on behalf of the Ephesians for the same blessings, using a little different terminology:

> For this reason I kneel before the Father, from whom his whole family in heaven and on earth derives its name. I pray that out of his glorious riches he may strengthen you with power through his Spirit in your inner being, so that Christ may dwell in your hearts through faith. And I pray that you, being rooted and established in love, may have power, together with all the saints, to grasp how wide and long and high and deep is the love of Christ, and to know this love that surpasses knowledge—that you may be filled to the measure of all the fullness of God. Now to him who is able to do immeasurably more than all we ask or imagine, according to his power that is at work within us, to him be glory in the church and in Christ Jesus throughout all generations, for ever and ever! Amen. (Ephesians 3:14-21)

If only Christ would dwell in our hearts by faith, we think. If only we would become more rooted and established in love. If only we had more power to grasp "how wide and long and high and deep is the love of Christ," a love "that surpasses knowledge." If only we might be filled with "all the fullness of God." If only . . . ? It is not a matter of "if only" potentialities. We have God's promise that what we ask for will be granted, for he "is able to do immeasurably more than all we ask or imagine, according to his power that is at work within us."

As we pray these prayers for ourselves and for our fellow Christians, we address God confidently but also humbly. He works where and when he pleases. He knows the right time for everything in our lives, and that includes granting us answers to our prayers for spiritual power. In the end, he alone will receive the glory, for we will realize that he alone is responsible for the insight we receive.

Paul prayed for the Colossians:

> For this reason, since the day we heard about you, we have not stopped praying for you and asking God to fill you with the knowledge of his will through all spiritual wisdom and understanding. And we pray this in order that you may live

> a life worthy of the Lord and may please him in every way:
> bearing fruit in every good work, growing in the knowledge
> of God, being strengthened with all power according to his
> glorious might so that you may have great endurance and
> patience, and joyfully giving thanks to the Father, who has
> qualified you to share in the inheritance of the saints in the
> kingdom of light. (Colossians 1:9-12)

Paul asked God to give his people "knowledge of his will
through all spiritual wisdom and understanding" so that we
"may live a life worthy of the Lord and may please him in
every way: bearing fruit in every good work."

In the following verses, Paul was praying for the fledgling
church in Thessalonica:

> Now may our God and Father himself and our Lord Jesus
> clear the way for us to come to you. May the Lord make your
> love increase and overflow for each other and for everyone
> else, just as ours does for you. May he strengthen your
> hearts so that you will be blameless and holy in the presence
> of our God and Father when our Lord Jesus comes with all
> his holy ones. (1 Thessalonians 3:11-13)

> May God himself, the God of peace, sanctify you through and
> through. May your whole spirit, soul and body be kept blame-
> less at the coming of our Lord Jesus Christ. The one who calls
> you is faithful and he will do it. (1 Thessalonians 5:23,24)

> May our Lord Jesus Christ himself and God our Father, who
> loved us and by his grace gave us eternal encouragement
> and good hope, encourage your hearts and strengthen you in
> every good deed and word. (2 Thessalonians 2:16,17)

One person wisely said, "If you cannot speak to a person
about God, then speak to God about that person." God alone
has the power to do what we cannot, that is, work directly on a
person's heart. In answer to our prayers, God will enable our
fellow Christians to understand the gospel better and better.
They will have deeper insights into the hope of their inheritance. And more and more they will live in service to God.

11

Special Examples, Part 1

Examples

In the previous chapters we looked at gospel motivation according to themes. In this chapter we will look at longer sections of Scripture and focus on the particular lack of sanctification the Bible writer was trying to correct and how he worked to correct it.

The ultimate goal of God's plan of salvation is to restore us to the perfection and fellowship we had with him in the Garden of Eden. Yet if that was all he wanted for us, he would have taken us to heaven as soon as we came to faith in Christ. Could God accomplish his plan if he did that? Not really. The Lord wants a body of believers to exist in this world so the faith can be passed down from one generation to the next. As children of God, we are called to be the light of the world and salt of the earth. Our own sanctification dovetails with God's plan for us, for our congregations, for the world, and, ultimately, for his own glory.

Accordingly, the Bible is not a dogmatics book, in which the teachings of the Christian faith are laid out in systematic order and in which sanctification is discussed particularly in its relation to justification. The New Testament is God's call to holiness in Christ and to holy living. He makes us his children and then calls us to live in line with what we are. Accordingly, much of the New Testament was written because there were problems in the church or because there was a need to strengthen a particular group of Christians. Even the so-called chief doctrinal book of the New Testament, Romans, was written to strengthen the Roman Christians so they could provide a base of support for Paul when he did mission work in Spain. Many of the beautiful Bible passages we learned in confirmation class, which were set in the context of a doctrinal topic, are actually found in passages that are teaching and encouraging sanctification. For example, many of the beautiful statements of Jesus recorded in the gospel of John were spoken in rebuke of the Pharisees and teachers of the law. In fact, most of John's gospel—and remember, John is the "apostle of love"—is comprised of Jesus rebuking and trying to correct his enemies.

The Bible is a book about living in holiness to the Lord. How we became holy in Christ is where it all starts. His victory over Satan and his forgiveness of our sins make us heirs of eternal life. We are called on to live lives as God's people. The world offers many alternatives and tries to force those alternatives on God's people through persecution of one sort or another. And so do the spiritual powers of darkness. They provide a myriad of other spirits to supplant the Holy Spirit. They take control of the leaders of nations who make false teachings the religion of the land and then make life intolerable for God's people.

In answer to this, Jesus and his writers urge us to hold on to our faith and live as God's people. They urge us to maintain our loyalty to Christ and his chosen apostles. They urge us to follow God's will. They tell us they are praying for us. And in the process, they provide a beautiful pattern for us when we do the same for our fellow believers. That pattern is what this present book is about. The Lutheran church has sometimes been charged with preaching more justification than sanctification. Sadly, some who are concerned about this solve the problem by talking more about morality, perhaps even cutting back on repeating the basic gospel message. But this problem, if it exists, is easily solved. Working through books of the Bible as they stand, submitting to their agenda and merely seeking to mine their treasures will provide a perfect balance of justification and sanctification. It provides much more, though. It provides a sense of that wonderful "pattern of sound teaching" (2 Timothy 1:13), where our faith in Christ predominates and where sanctification issues are exposed and corrected as only the Holy Spirit can do it.

In this chapter and the next, we will look at a few examples of this pattern. We start with Ephesians 5:22-33. I won't write out all these verses. You may wish to read them before you go on. This is the section where Paul tells husbands and wives to submit to each other and then spells out how each should do this.

It is not Paul's intent merely to outline a program of living. Nor does he merely state God's will. Rather, he chooses ways of discussing the issue that are drawn from the gospel of God's grace. In other words, he recognizes the issue (and the problem) and then chooses one aspect of the gospel message appropriate for it. Here he deals with the roles of men and women. Since the roles of men and women deal with (1) a relationship and (2) a relationship in which there is a certain hierarchy (although that is too cold a term), Paul sets the marriage of a man and a woman against the backdrop of the relationship of Christ and the church.

Paul begins with a few words to wives. He tells wives to submit to their husbands. Many wives don't want to do this. Yet when wives read these words, they see that their submission goes deeper than a forced submission to the sometimes arbitrary human will of their husbands. Paul pictures the relationship of the church to Christ. Christ is the head; the church is his body. When a wife thinks of this relationship, she sees a beautiful picture in which headship and submission can exist without any feelings of animosity or arbitrary superiority. No member of Christ's church sees Christ as an arbitrary, self-centered head. Every member of the church willingly submits to Christ because he or she knows that Christ gave up his life for the church and wants nothing but the church's good. Christ is the perfect head. Husbands are never perfect heads. Sin precludes that. But Paul tells the wife that she should submit to her head with the same devotion that the church submits to Christ. This evokes willingness in the wife to submit to her less-than-perfect husband, for she certainly is willing to submit to Christ.

Paul turns to the husband and has much more to say to him. The picture of Christ loving the church creates a true understanding of headship. The husband often looks to the wife to generate feelings of love in the marriage. But imagine this: If Christ waited for the church to initiate the love in his relationship with her, he would be waiting forever. Christ must lead. He did lead. And the church follows. If there is a lack of love in the marriage, the husband should first look at himself. That said, Paul reminds us of the great sacrifice Christ made for his church. Husbands are to love their wives in the same way, sacrificing themselves for their wives.

Christ did more. He sacrificed himself for his church to make her members into something they were not. He made his church holy. He did this through Baptism (as we saw so clearly in Romans 6), which joins us with Christ in his death and life. He made the church beautiful, and then he presented her to himself in all her perfection and joined her to him. The church (and all her members) has become part of Christ, his body, which he nourishes and cares for. This symbolizes the union between a husband and wife. The wife is the husband's body, and he is her head; she draws care and nurture from him.

In this section on husbands and wives, the Lord actually dedicates more words to describing Christ and his church. Christian husbands and wives know what Christ means to them. They know how Christ loves the church, and they understand what it means that the church submits to Christ. They also know how Christ acts toward the church as the church's head, doing nothing but good for her. It is this union—Christ and his church—that drives Paul's discussion. It infuses everything he says about the relationship of husbands and wives under God with the gospel. This is true gospel motivation. The gospel sets the tone, gives the pattern, and supplies the reason for how husbands and wives are to deal with each other.

What is practical?

At this point let's pause and think about what Paul is doing in Ephesians 5. Paul here is talking about a very practical subject. How Paul approaches marriage is interesting in view of what our modern culture is crying out for because of its problems with marriage and family issues. The cry today is for practical, easily applied advice. Congregations, wanting to grow, find almost overwhelming the desire to use this need to bring people into association with their church. So they offer practical seminars and programs for the community. Since the home and family in Western culture is disintegrating and many are crying out for answers, churches find ready audiences of husbands and wives seeking answers to their desperate questions about their married lives together.

The comments that follow are meant to lead us to think about what it means for church leaders to be "practical" in view of Paul's discussion in Ephesians 5 and other places. I believe there is a tension between what is practical in the world's definition and what is practical in Christian terms. When well-meaning seminar leaders look to Scripture for practical advice, they stumble onto sections of Scripture that contain good advice, to be sure. But they also find the Bible writer's entire discussion based on the gospel and how life should reflect the Christian hope, not just the desire for a better earthly life.

One person made a helpful distinction between two kinds of knowledge. He distinguished between "good things" and "God's things."

Good things are just that, good pieces of knowledge and understanding that one person may gain and pass on to another. Through the work of observing and counseling others and through the writings of particularly wise people, we gather a good deal of knowledge and understanding about how things work. We know what things contribute to our temporal happiness and well-being and what things harm them. The church is often viewed as a dispenser of good things: wisdom from God found in the Bible, put into practice in the Christian community and proven to produce happiness and well-being.

God's things, though, are different. God's things relate to our salvation. God's things stem from a wisdom that is not based on experience. God's wisdom centers on the death and life of Jesus. It centers on Baptism, on Christ's righteousness, and on the fact that we are free from the law. God's things center on the new life created in us. God's things focus on living in service to God.

The desire to hear good things and put them into practice stems from human desires. The desire to hear God's things begins with wanting to hear about Christ, and the desire to do the right thing stems from a desire to live in line with what we have become, God's redeemed children.

The work of the church will invariably entail dispensing good things and God's things. Counseling will always include practical advice on how to deal with the issues that arise in marriage and the family. Christian love leads us to help in whatever way we can, whether that is relief aid for starvation victims or relief aid to families starving for peace.

But is this the work Christ has given his church? Can good things and God's things actually coexist in a person's ministry? I would answer yes and no. Yes, because the Christian will do everything he or she can to help others with whatever needs they have, including marriage and family needs. But I would also answer no, because the church is given the work of proclaiming God's message of salvation and leading people to live for him. The church must be careful that in its preaching and teaching and even counseling it strives to keep that mission foremost in its mind.

So what does it mean to be practical? Sad to say, in the minds of many, practical religion means religion stripped of theology. It means dispensing how-to advice. It means counseling to one's individual, personal, and unique needs, rather than preaching global truths that deal with God's salvation for the whole world and that deal especially with Christians—sin, forgiveness, the new creation, and living lives of love.

We might ask, what does God consider to be truly practical? From Scripture we learn that his definition of practicality is not quite the same as the world's. The heart of practicality can be summarized in Paul's statement, "Whether you eat or drink or whatever you do, do it all for the glory of God" (1 Corinthians 10:31). What is to God's glory? God is glorified when he brings people from darkness to light, extends his rule of grace, and leads people into heaven. God is glorified when people honor, love, and obey him and worship him by following his commands. God is glorified when people seek to grow in Christ, seeking first his kingdom and resting content to have God give them what he wants to give them according to his time schedule.

Everything we have seen about gospel motivation has presupposed that the gospel was the most important thing to Paul's readers. If it was not, then everything Paul said fell on deaf ears and God has preserved Paul's words only to be culled for some tidbit of practical truth that can be extracted from it. For example, is Paul talking about husbands and wives in Ephesians 5? Is he giving married people practical advice for living? Again, yes and no. Yes in the sense that Paul is discussing something concrete that I should do in my life. But what he writes was not written to help my earthly well-being but to teach me how to live in light of my faith in Christ, his living relationship with the church. How can anyone offer a practical marriage class to non-Christians in the community and use Ephesians 5? It is beyond me.

Let's ask the question another way. Is God concerned about our practical happiness and well-being? If you were the Lord, how would you show your concern to someone you love, knowing that the brief and momentary time we spend on this earth is a grain of sand compared with the eternity that stretches out before us? If you truly loved that person, you would be concerned about whether he or she navigates this life success-fully, interpreting the word *successfully* as avoiding anything that would take away that person's faith. You certainly would want that person to be happy in his or her marriage. But there may come a time when God may not want a person to have a happy marriage because marital problems are part of his chastening work. Or the Lord may know that the suffering a person must go through is necessary for his or her faith—perhaps a time of humbling or a time when he is dealing with the other spouse's sinful nature. That is truly practical. That's the Bible's definition of practical.

Finally, how would you define *practical* in light of every-thing we have seen so far in our look at gospel motivation? How practical is our baptism in terms of Romans 6? How practical is our knowledge that we have received Christ's righteousness and are slaves of righteousness? How practical is the teaching that we are free from the law? How practical is Paul's discussion of the new man and the old man? How prac-tical is Paul's statement that if we put to death the misdeeds of the body, we will live? How practical is the Bible's teaching of hell and of heaven?

Is there anything on earth that is more practical than these truths? People who have hope only for this life may or may not be influenced by the problems of their lives to seek advice and apply it. Sick people keep on eating as they did before they became sick, even though they know their eating habits will eventually kill them. Alcoholics continue to drink in spite of the harm it causes their bodies, jobs, and home life. Men continue to view pornography in spite of the harm such self-indulgence brings into their lives. You can describe the sin and expose its consequences and still the sinful nature will commit those sins, even to the point of sadistic self-destruction.

Only what transcends this life is truly practical. Only the truth of God's eternal judgment on the sinner and his gracious redemption in Christ truly mean something. If this life and our happiness here is all there is to live for, then the sinful nature will always win the battle as to how this life should be lived. If morality is merely a personal thing, warranting reward or punishment in this life, the sinful nature will always win the argument as to whether a little pain is worth the pleasure of lust and sinful ambition. If self-interest is pitted against love and kindness to others, the sinful nature will always choose self-interest, yes, even if it comes in the form of "service to others."

Only life in Christ transcends the risk of temporal punishment for immorality and our inherent selfishness. It lifts us above the "practical" desires of the world and leads us to think of life in view of God and his glory. Such a view of life can only come through realizing our sin (another theological concept, but so practical in the ultimate sense) and repenting of it. It comes only by submitting to Christ's righteousness and finding our hope there. It comes only through the power of the Holy Spirit working through the gospel of our death and life in Christ. The sinful nature can only be stopped when in Christ the law's demands are removed from contact with the lusts of the sinful nature. Only then can I serve in a new and willing spirit. The church can only carry out its mission and be truly practical if it relegates itself to preaching the law and the gospel. Every other message is a Band-Aid for a cancer patient.

Examples, continued

We should get back to the theme of this chapter, namely, instances of how the writers of the New Testament weave the gospel into all their admonitions and encouragements.

One of the most striking sections of the New Testament for our purposes is a series of chapters in 1 Corinthians. Those familiar with 1 Corinthians know it to be a letter written to a congregation that had a lot of problems. The Lord had richly blessed the Corinthians, but they did not make the jump from pagan thinking to godly thinking overnight, at least not in every corner of their lives.

In his first letter to the Corinthians, Paul addresses a number of problems, spanning chapters 5 through 14. He moves from one issue to the next. What is striking is the pattern he follows. He presents the issue, and then he follows with some aspect of the gospel or with some way the gospel has had an impact on the Corinthians' lives. We will take the issues in order. You may want to read chapters 5 through 11. (Add 12 through 14 if you wish. We'll touch briefly on those chapters.)

In chapter 5 Paul addresses a sin that a member of the church was committing. A man was committing incest with his mother (probably his stepmother). The sin was out in the open, and the members of the congregation knew about it. They were also being rather open-minded about the sin, and they refused to take a stand against it. Paul rebuked them. He said, "Hand this man over to Satan, so that the sinful nature may be destroyed and his spirit saved on the day of the Lord" (verse 5). At this point Paul injected the gospel into his discussion. He did it in a way that fit the problem he was working with. Not all the Corinthians were engaged in the actual sin, of course. But they were implicating themselves in it by not doing anything about it. So how should Paul bring the gospel into the mix? Remember, he has already rebuked the Corinthians with the law. Now he wants to fill their hearts with gospel motivation. Paul is not just concerned about the immoral nature of the sin, the effects the sin might have on the people committing it, or even about the spiritual life of the Corinthian church. Paul knows that if they continue to condone the sin, the gospel will no longer mean anything to them and eventually they will lose it.

Paul's approach to the problem contains three elements (1 Corinthians 5:6-8). First, he uses a few short phrases designed to remind his readers of a time in the Old Testament when the gospel shone clearly in the lives of God's people. This was the Passover. Second, he states that the Passover was fulfilled when Jesus died for their sins. Third, he shows how the Passover Feast (the festival Israel was to follow in the days after the Passover itself) was fulfilled in their lives when they came to know Jesus.

Paul encouraged them in a masterful way. The people of Israel were to get rid of yeast in their homes prior to the Passover. When the day came, they were to make unleavened bread and eat it with the lamb that had been killed earlier that day. A little yeast left in the home could potentially work its way into the dough and spoil the unleavened bread. Yeast was clearly a picture of sin. When the people of Israel rid their homes of yeast, in their minds they were purifying their lives so they could celebrate the Passover. The unleavened bread symbolized repentance and a home that had rid itself of sin.

Paul wove all these ideas together. Jesus, our Passover Lamb, has been sacrificed. We have the forgiveness of sin. We are to rid our lives of the leaven of sin and be pure, just "as [we] really are." In other words, in our lives we are to be what we have become in Christ. Then as we eat the Passover festival every day anew, we are not to eat it with the sinful bread we used to eat but with unleavened bread, that is, with sincere hearts, doing what is in line with the truth.

Using images from the first Passover, Paul sets Christ, the Passover Lamb, in the middle of the problem. Paul is confident that the Corinthians' love for Christ will shape their hearts to follow God's will.

In 1 Corinthians 6, Paul addresses lawsuits among believers (verses 1-11) and sexual immorality (verses 12-20). The Corinthians were dragging fellow Christians before secular courts and leveling charges against them. Paul rebuked them in a number of ways. He finished his rebuke by getting to the heart of the problem—greed and wickedness. He reminded the Corinthians:

> Do you not know that the wicked will not inherit the kingdom of God? Do not be deceived: Neither the sexually immoral nor idolaters nor adulterers nor male prostitutes nor homosexual offenders nor thieves nor the greedy nor drunkards nor slanderers nor swindlers will inherit the kingdom of God. (1 Corinthians 6:9,10)

But then, after this scathing rebuke, Paul reminds them that they have been delivered from these sins and their inevitable end.

> That is what some of you were. But you were washed, you were sanctified, you were justified in the name of the Lord Jesus Christ and by the Spirit of our God. (1 Corinthians 6:11)

The gospel is closely packed into these verses. In one short verse, we have the message of Baptism, the forgiveness of sins, God's declaration of justification ("not guilty"), and reminders that all this came through Jesus Christ, and that we have received the Holy Spirit, who has worked all of these blessings in us.

In 1 Corinthians 6:12-20, Paul addresses sexual immorality. The sin of prostitution was common in Corinth as in most of the ancient world. The sexual act had deep religious significance. Many Corinthians believed that when the gods saw humans having sexual intercourse, they were moved to make the earth fertile and bless humans with the gift of children. Ingrained patterns of behavior were hard to break, especially in regard to actions that had formerly been considered to be a religious duty.

Paul knew he had to rebuke the Corinthians. He did, but he also wove the gospel into his rebuke, again, in a way especially tailored to the problem. Since the sin had to do with their bodies, Paul addressed the issue from that standpoint. Paul pointed out the relation of our bodies to our Lord. The body is "for the Lord, and the Lord for the body" (verse 13). Christ and his Father have come to live in us. For this reason we are to use our bodies in service to the Lord: "Offer yourselves to God, as those who have been brought from death to life; and offer the parts of your body to him as instruments of righteousness" (Romans 6:13). In 1 Corinthians 6:17, Paul reminds the Corinthians that in Christ they have the wonderful blessing of being united in spirit with God. Why give up that unity by being joined with a prostitute? In verses 19 and 20, Paul reminds us that God's Spirit is living in us. God gave us his Spirit because Christ gave up his own life to make us people who belong to God. Our union with Christ precludes union with sin.

In 1 Corinthians 7, Paul answers questions the Corinthians had asked about marriage. Paul does not weave the gospel into his answers as he did in the previous two chapters. But it is clear that the gospel and the Corinthians' relationship with Christ is still at the heart of his thoughts. Husbands and wives should not deprive each other, lest Satan tempt them (7:5). Christians should not divorce their non-Christian spouses, because if they do, their spouses and children will not have the presence of the gospel in their lives. A Christian is so concerned about the faith of his or her children and spouse that he or she is willing to remain in a difficult marriage for the sake of their spiritual welfare (7:14).

Christians should be content to remain in whatever situation they were in when they came to faith. This could apply to marriage or to circumcision. Slaves should be content to remain slaves if it is God's will, because in Christ they are free. Freemen should not look down on their slaves, because through faith they themselves have become slaves to God and to the righteousness they have by faith (7:20-24). Even the decision whether or not to get married is to be guided by how this impacts one's work for the Lord.

In 1 Corinthians 8, Paul addresses eating food sacrificed to idols. Most modern readers, especially Western readers, probably won't relate to this problem. Here's what was happening. A citizen of an ancient heathen city worshiped his or her god by bringing a sacrifice to the temple. The sacrifice might be a lamb or goat or cow. Often we imagine the priest leading this sacrifice to the altar, killing it, cutting it apart, and burning the whole thing. That would only be partially correct. Some of the sacrifices were probably burned up completely. But in many cases, only parts of the sacrifice were burned, perhaps because the priest thought the parts were what the god preferred. Much of the sacrifice remained after the ceremony was over. A good portion of the meat was sent to butcher shops adjacent to the temple. The money the people paid to buy the meat would go to support the temple. It was an ongoing bake sale of sorts.

If you had just come to faith in Christ, what would you have done if this were the only place, or perhaps the most convenient place, to buy meat? That's the situation behind the issue Paul had to address. Some were buying and eating this meat in good conscience, realizing that a false god was a figment of people's imagination, prompted by Satan. Others, however, felt that an idol, a figment of sinful imagination or not, was still associated with sins against the First Commandment. They felt guilt by association and refused to eat this meat. If they went to the home of someone who served such meat, they might think, "Well, it is probably okay to eat this. My conscience feels uneasy about joining in, but I'll eat it anyway." When a Christian sins against his conscience like this, he sins, even if what he is doing is not sinful.

You can probably guess how Paul would advise in this matter. Read the following verses to find out. For our purposes, however, we are interested if and how Paul weaves the gospel into his instructions. He does not disappoint us. Once again, he weaves the gospel into the section in a way appropriate to the theme. Read how Paul begins the section, and also read verses 4, 7, and 10. The main words are *know* and *knowledge*. The problem originated between some people who knew something (it's okay to eat this food) and some who did not know this, or at least did not accept it in their hearts and consciences. So Paul focuses on knowledge:

> Now about food sacrificed to idols: We know that we all possess knowledge. Knowledge puffs up, but love builds up. The man who thinks he knows something does not yet know as he ought to know. But the man who loves God is known by God. (1 Corinthians 8:1-3)

Paul begins with the concept of knowledge. Then he immediately shifts the thought to love, because love, not knowledge, is important. Knowledge can tear Christians apart. Love will always bind them together. So far, so good. But note the beautiful touch of Paul's final words in verse 3. There is a very important kind of knowledge, Paul says. It's the knowledge God has of us, that he knows us in Christ and views us as his children in Christ. Tracking Paul's thought backwards, he points out that those who know that they are known by God will reflect God's love. Love will direct them to handle the situation correctly. In a concise way, the whole issue is introduced and resolved. Understand knowledge in the right way, Paul says, and then love your fellow Christian (who may not be on your level of knowledge) because you know that God loves you in Christ (in spite of the fact that you are not at all on Christ's level).

As we work through this section, we see other bits of gospel woven into Paul's words. He reminds us that if we selfishly force our knowledge on one of God's children, we will destroy someone "for whom Christ died" (verse 11). He also focuses on the true knowledge that binds us together with fellow Christians. There is one Father who made us and directs our lives; there is "but one Lord, Jesus Christ" who created all things and died for us so that we might live in him. This way of speaking helps us see our fellow Christians for who they are, namely, people who are one with us in the Lord.

First Corinthians 9 is a bit different than the preceding chapters. Some in the Corinthian congregation were judging Paul and criticizing the way he carried out his ministry. In his defense, Paul speaks about the purity and sincerity of his heart when he preached the gospel to them. He explains how the gospel is continually motivating him to give his entire life in its service. We won't look at this section in detail, but one verse summarizes everything he says: "I do all this for the sake of the gospel, that I may share in its blessings" (1 Corinthians 9:23).

Citizens of a Greek city-state like Corinth were brought up worshiping idols. It was nothing strange to them. The temptations they faced would be equivalent to what a Japanese Christian today would face at conversion. If one spouse in the marriage came to faith, he or she would still go to bed at night looking at his or her spouse's little Shinto shrine in the bedroom or perhaps a shrine to Buddha in the hallway. Secular and sacred would be mixed, and not going to an idol celebration for conscience reasons would be like taking a stand against a Fourth of July celebration in the United States.

The temptation to bow down before idols was strong in Corinth. The comparison of an idol festival with a Fourth of July celebration breaks down, however, when we realize what idol festivals entailed. When the gods were worshiped with temple prostitution, you can imagine the further compromises Christians were forced to make if they did give in to pressure to attend a feast.

This is the situation Paul addresses in 1 Corinthians 10. There are a lot of law warnings in verses 1 to 13, where Paul draws from Israel's history. But there is also gospel woven in.

For example, Paul urges the Corinthians to remember God's blessings: Christ himself, Baptism, and the Lord's Supper:

> I do not want you to be ignorant of the fact, brothers, that our forefathers were all under the cloud and that they all passed through the sea. They were all baptized into Moses in the cloud and in the sea. They all ate the same spiritual food and drank the same spiritual drink; for they drank from the spiritual rock that accompanied them, and that rock was Christ. Nevertheless, God was not pleased with most of them; their bodies were scattered over the desert. (1 Corinthians 10:1-5)

Look at how creative Paul is. He joins New Testament Christians with Old Testament believers so he can use the sins of people in the Old Testament to warn the Corinthians against idolatry. The Israelites were baptized into Moses, a man in service to the Lord on behalf of Israel. We also have been baptized into Jesus' death and resurrection. The Israelites ate spiritual food—manna from heaven—and they drank spiritual drink—water flowing from dry rocks. We also eat spiritual food and drink spiritual drink—the Lord's Supper. They had Christ, the Angel of the Lord, accompanying them. We also are joined to Christ by faith, and he accompanies us through life. In a masterful way, Paul links us with the Old Testament people of God and reminds us of the blessings we have received. Now he can warn the Corinthians and us against idolatry. The Israelites rejected God's blessings, and God punished them. We should never follow their pattern.

Beginning in 1 Corinthians 10:14, where he addresses idol feasts directly, Paul follows his pattern by placing the gospel of the Lord's Supper right in the middle of the problem. Paul begins by reminding the Corinthians of what they ate and drank in the Lord's Supper:

> I speak to sensible people; judge for yourselves what I say. Is not the cup of thanksgiving for which we give thanks a participation in the blood of Christ? And is not the bread that we break a participation in the body of Christ? (1 Corinthians 10:15,16)

The problem Paul is addressing has to do with eating and drinking at an idol feast. So his theme is going to be just that, eating and drinking at a feast. Christians also have a feast, the Lord's feast, to which the Lord has invited us. When we drink wine at his feast, we drink the blood of Christ. When we eat bread at his feast, we eat the body of Christ. We also join ourselves with fellow Christians, for when we eat and drink we participate in the one Christ.

Paul applies all this in these words: "You cannot drink the cup of the Lord and the cup of demons too; you cannot have a part in both the Lord's table and the table of demons" (1 Corinthians 10:21). Paul's warning is not a bare warning based on the Ten Commandments. It is a warning based on the incongruity of doing two opposite things at the same time. Such a thing will "arouse the Lord's jealousy."

Returning to the issue of eating food from the butcher shops located around the idol temples, Paul writes, "Whether you eat or drink or whatever you do, do it all for the glory of God" (1 Corinthians 10:31).

We have already discussed chapter 11 to some extent in our section on the gospel of the sacraments. The Corinthians were having trouble in their worship services; specifically, the rich were looking down on the poor and segregating themselves from them. So what does Paul do? He reminds them again of the Lord's Supper that both the rich and poor celebrate together. This will have the effect of clearing up the problems from within, that is, hearts motivated by the gospel of forgiveness contained in the Lord's Supper will enable the Corinthians to deal with fellow Christians in love.

First Corinthians 12 and 14 deal with spiritual gifts. We won't be looking at these chapters in detail. Please note one thing, however. Right in the middle of his discussion on the proper use of spiritual gifts—which can stir up pride and strife if not used in a God-pleasing way—Paul places what has become one of the most famous chapters in Scripture, the chapter on love. This chapter deals with brotherly love in Christ, the kind of love that will guide and shape the way Christians use their spiritual gifts. God's gifts, Paul says, mean nothing unless they are used in a spirit of love, which can only come from the knowledge of God's love for us.

We will touch on a few more special examples in the next chapter.

12

Special Examples, Part 2

We conclude our review with a few more special examples of how Paul weaves together the gospel and encouragement to godly living.

Colossians 2:20–3:17

The last verses in Colossians 2 and the first 17 verses of Colossians 3 present some of the most beautiful encouragements to sanctification in Scripture. We will be breaking into Paul's thought in midstream, but 2:20 is a good place to start.

At the end of chapter 2, Paul distinguishes between the "basic principles of this world," that is, the way the people of the world strive to become holy, and God's way to holiness. He writes:

> Since **you died with Christ to the basic principles of this world,** *why, as though you still belonged to it, do you submit to its rules: "Do not handle! Do not taste! Do not touch!"?* These are all destined to perish with use, because they are based on human commands and teachings. Such regulations indeed have an appearance of wisdom, with their self-imposed worship, their false humility and their harsh treatment of the body, but they lack any value in restraining sensual indulgence. (Colossians 2:20-23)

In verse 20 Paul says the same thing that he said in Romans 6 and 7. We died with Christ. We are living new lives in service to him. This new life dominates us. One of the ways we serve the Lord is by avoiding the world's methods of "self-improvement." The world works with rules. The world operates on the basis of human reason and teachings. Yes, Paul says, these rules appear wise. The world's worship seems reasonable, especially when it is accompanied by humility and harsh treatment of the body. But these rules do nothing to motivate and enable a truly God-pleasing life.

How does a God-pleasing life come about? It comes about when we know we have died with Christ to sin and the curse of the law. It happens when we remember the counterpart of our death in Christ, namely, our resurrection with him and the fact that we are now in heaven with him.

> **Since, then, you have been raised with Christ,** *set your hearts on things above, where Christ is seated at the right hand of God. Set your minds on things above, not on earthly things.* **For you died, and your life is now hidden with Christ in God. When Christ, who is your life, appears, then you also will appear with him in glory.** (Colossians 3:1-4)

When we truly take to heart what Paul says here, we cannot help but be launched into a life of service to God. We have been "raised with Christ." The Lord with whom we have been raised has ascended into heaven and now is "seated at the right hand of God." Spiritually, that's where we are too. As Paul puts it, we are "hidden with Christ in God." Then follows a rather surprising statement. When Christ appears, we "also will appear with him in glory." The Bible tells us that when we see Christ coming in the heavens, we should lift up our heads because our redemption is drawing near (Luke 21:28). Here in Colossians, however, Paul says that when Christ comes again, we will appear "with" him in glory. We physically live here on earth, but we are also spiritually in heaven with the Lord. Sometimes Christians are asked where they want to be when Jesus returns. The fact that we are with him in heaven right now affords a fine answer to that question.

At this point Paul tells us what to do:

> Put to death, therefore, whatever belongs to your earthly nature: sexual immorality, impurity, lust, evil desires and greed, which is idolatry. Because of these, the wrath of God is coming. You used to walk in these ways, in the life you **once lived.** *But now you must rid yourselves of all such things as these: anger, rage, malice, slander, and filthy language from your lips. Do not lie to each other,* **since you have taken off your old self with its practices and have put on the new self, which is being renewed in knowledge in the image of its Creator.** (Colossians 3:5-10)

Because we are with Christ, who is in heaven, we are to put to death the sins that belong to the sinful nature. Notice the gospel elements woven into this section. The life we "once lived," we live no longer. We have "taken off" the old self with its practices and have "put on the new self." This is not something we *should* do but something *we have done* already. It's a status we enjoy because we have died and risen with Christ. The old self is gone. The new self is here, and by God's power we are being "renewed in knowledge in the image of its Creator."

In the following verses, Paul continually weaves the gospel into his exhortations:

> Here there is no Greek or Jew, circumcised or uncircumcised, barbarian, Scythian, slave or free, but **Christ is all, and is in all.** Therefore, **as God's chosen people, holy and dearly loved,** *clothe yourselves with compassion, kindness, humility, gentleness and patience. Bear with each other and forgive whatever grievances you may have against one*

another. Forgive **as the Lord forgave you.** *And over all these virtues put on love, which binds them all together in perfect unity. Let the peace of Christ rule in your hearts,* **since as members of one body you were called to peace.** *And be thankful.* *Let the word of Christ dwell in you* richly as you teach and admonish one another with all wisdom, and as you sing psalms, hymns and spiritual songs with gratitude in your hearts to God. And whatever you do, whether in word or deed, *do it all* **in the name of the Lord Jesus,** *giving thanks to God the Father through him.* (Colossians 3:11-17)

We are not to view social distinctions as a reason for segregation. Why? Because all that we have stems from one source, Christ, and he is living in all of us. We are to clothe ourselves with God-pleasing virtues because we are "God's chosen people, holy and dearly loved" by the Lord. We are to forgive because "the Lord forgave you." We are to live in peace with one another because "as members of one body you were called to peace." The Word of God is to dwell in us "richly," a word reminding us of the rich promises that are found in that Word. We give thanks to God and do everything we do "in the name of the Lord Jesus," that is, because we are joined with him and experience his rich blessings.

2 Corinthians 8 and 9

Annual stewardship programs are important. And if we follow Paul's pattern, we will weave the gospel into our encouragements to give, just as we weave it into all our encouragements to sanctified living. Second Corinthians 8 and 9 is perhaps the most important section in the Bible on Christian giving.

Paul encouraged the Corinthians to give generously to the offering he was taking for the needy believers in Jerusalem. His appeal flowed from a spirit of love and concern for all involved: the believers in Jerusalem, who so desperately needed the offering; the Corinthians, who needed to give; and the Thessalonians, whose giving was spurred by the promises the Corinthians made about the offerings they would give. Toward the beginning of chapter 8, Paul writes:

> *I am not commanding you, but I want to test the sincerity of your love* by comparing it with the earnestness of others. **For you know the grace of our Lord Jesus Christ, that though he was rich, yet for your sakes he became poor, so that you through his poverty might become rich.** (2 Corinthians 8:8,9)

Verse 9 is well known and is often used in stewardship programs. Sometimes we use this passage to preach the gospel or to teach people why they should give. There is nothing really wrong in using this verse to teach people why they should give. Paul, however, does not really use it like that. He does not give this jewel of a gospel passage to the Corinthians because of a lack of knowledge but because they already know this truth.

Paul had just told them how willing and generous the Thessalonians were. Whenever you use someone's good example to spur someone else toward love and service, you give the latter a test. By using the Thessalonians' good example, Paul was testing the Corinthians. He was testing the sincerity of *their love*. That's gospel motivation. Paul is reminding the Corinthians of their love for God and for their fellow Christians, both based on God's love for them. By using the Thessalonians as an example, Paul gives the Corinthians' love a chance to rise to the surface and show itself.

How can Paul be sure the Corinthians have such love in their hearts? He knows that they know "the grace of our Lord Jesus Christ," who gave up his riches and became poor so that through his poverty they might become rich. What a gracious and beautiful way of speaking to people he is trying to encourage! He doesn't say, "Remember this . . . !" Rather—and without a hint of patronizing—he says, "I know you remember this. . . . That's why I can test you, and that's why I am confident you will respond in a God-pleasing way." This is true gospel motivation. (Also note how Paul shaped the proclamation of the gospel so it fit neatly with the subject of giving.)

Paul ends his encouragement with lofty gospel words:

> God is able to make all grace abound to you, so that in all things at all times, having all that you need, you will

abound in every good work. As it is written: "He has scattered abroad his gifts to the poor; his righteousness endures forever." Now he who supplies seed to the sower and bread for food will also supply and increase your store of seed and will enlarge the harvest of your righteousness. You will be made rich in every way so that you can be generous on every occasion, and through us your generosity will result in thanksgiving to God. This service that you perform is not only supplying the needs of God's people but is also overflowing in many expressions of thanks to God. Because of the service by which you have proved yourselves, men will praise God for the obedience that accompanies your confession of the gospel of Christ, and for your generosity in sharing with them and with everyone else. And in their prayers for you their hearts will go out to you, because of the surpassing grace God has given you. Thanks be to God for his indescribable gift! (2 Corinthians 9:8-15)

Here is the spirit of a man who wants only the good of God's church and who relies on God to supply everything the church needs to be a blessing to the world.

Paul reminds the Corinthians that God will make his grace overflow in their lives so "you will abound in every good work." Those simple words remind the Corinthians that they want to perform every good work. There's no question about it. God's righteousness, that is, his faithfulness to his covenant of love to his people, will never cease. He will continue to scatter his gifts to the poor so the poor can be rich in good works for the benefit of the church. The Corinthians would, in fact, produce a harvest of righteousness, that is, they will want to be part of God's righteous activity toward his people.

When the Corinthians' harvest of righteousness is "tasted" by the saints in Jerusalem, they will thank God for giving the Corinthians the grace of being able to give. In all this everyone is blessed, and God receives thanks for fulfilling his promises to bless his people.

Here is a case in which the gospel is not so much used as a reason to give but as a doxology of praise, which cannot but inspire the Corinthians to give their hearts to the Lord. This is gracious speech in the true sense of the term. It is enjoyable to listen to, and it is a goal to strive for in our speech. (Read the book of Philemon for another example of this kind of speech.)

Ephesians 4:29–5:10

The following verses from Ephesians carry many general admonitions and are infused with the gospel at every turn. Look at all the couplets of law instruction and gospel motivation:

> Do not let any unwholesome talk come out of your mouths, but only what is helpful for building others up according to their needs, that it may benefit those who listen. And *do not grieve the Holy Spirit of God,* **with whom you were sealed for the day of redemption.** *Get rid of all bitterness, rage and anger, brawling and slander, along with every form of malice. Be kind and compassionate to one another, forgiving each other,* **just as in Christ God forgave you.**
>
> *Be imitators of God, therefore,* **as dearly loved children** *and live a life of love,* **just as Christ loved us and gave himself up for us as a fragrant offering and sacrifice to God.** *But among you there must not be even a hint of sexual immorality, or of any kind of impurity, or of greed,* **because these are improper for God's holy people.** *Nor should there be obscenity, foolish talk or coarse joking,* **which are out of place,** *but rather thanksgiving.* For of this you can be sure: No immoral, impure or greedy person—such a man is an idolater—has any inheritance in **the kingdom of Christ and of God.**
>
> Let no one deceive you with empty words, for because of such things God's wrath comes on those who are disobedient. *Therefore do not be partners with them.* **For you were once darkness, but now you are light in the Lord.** *Live as children of light (for the fruit of the light consists in all goodness, righteousness and truth) and find out what pleases the Lord.* (Ephesians 4:29–5:10)

Do not grieve the Holy Spirit—by him you were sealed for the day when your bodies will be redeemed. Get rid of bitterness, rage, anger, and other hateful emotions, and forgive one another—just as God forgave you. Live a life of love—just as Christ loved us and gave himself up for us as a sacrifice.

There must not be a hint of sexual immorality among you, or impurity or greed—these are improper for God's holy people. Do not be partners with those who are disobedient—you were once in darkness, but now you live in the light of the Lord— live as children of light.

Granted, not every section of Scripture is filled with these pairs running together so closely through an extended section, but some are. And where there are extended sections of instruction without a lot of gospel, a section of gospel motivation has already come before or is not far behind.

1 Peter 1:13–2:24

From the context of 1 Peter, we see that the Christians in Asia Minor to whom Peter wrote were suffering persecution. Peter encouraged his readers to remain firm in the faith. In the process, Peter gives us a wonderful example of a Christian pastor weaving the gospel into his admonitions. I will not print out every verse of this section. You may wish to read 1 Peter 1:13–2:24 on your own.

In the face of suffering, Peter encouraged his readers to "prepare your minds for action" and to "be self-controlled." This encouragement leads into a promise of future glory. They were to "set [their] hope fully on the grace to be given [them] when Jesus Christ is revealed." Hope, grace, Christ's appearing: these are all messages of the gospel, which alone could prepare them for action and give them self-control.

As obedient children, Peter reminds them to put away the evil desires they had before they came to faith. They were to be holy, as God is holy. Here is much encouragement to live a sanctified life. But notice the gospel touch that sets the pace for the passage. Peter was writing to "obedient children." Two thoughts are woven together in this beautiful two-word phrase. His readers were "children," children of God, who loved them. Peter also saw that they were obedient children. We ask, "How can he call them obedient children? After all, they hadn't yet had a chance to do what Peter tells them to do." True, but Peter knew the Holy Spirit was living in them, and he knew that through the Spirit they were putting to death the misdeeds of the flesh. Peter was not ingratiating himself to them so they would follow his instructions. He was simply stating a fact. They were new creatures through their death and life to God in Christ.

In verse 17 Peter warns his readers that they should call on the Father who judges all people impartially and that they should live in reverent fear of his justice. But he weaves the gospel into his admonition by reminding them that they are "strangers" in this world, which, in turn, reminds them of their citizenship in heaven. Then in verses 18 and 19, Peter launches into a gospel passage that every confirmation-age child memorizes:

> You know that it was not with perishable things such as silver or gold that you were redeemed from the empty way of life handed down to you from your forefathers, but with the precious blood of Christ, a lamb without blemish or defect. (1 Peter 1:18,19)

Peter encourages his readers to "love one another deeply, from the heart" (verse 22). He knows his encouragement will not be in vain, for his readers have been purified by obeying the truth (another way of saying they believed God's truth about Christ) and already have sincere love for their brothers. Again we see an odd combination of phrases. Peter tells his readers to love, and then he tells them they can do that because they already love their brothers in faith. However, we do understand his way of speaking. His readers know the love of Christ, and they love because God loved them first. But because they still have their old sinful flesh that can only hate, they need to be reminded of what God has made them to be, and they need to be encouraged to live according to the new life God has created in them.

After encouraging them to love, Peter reminds them of their rebirth through the living and enduring Word of God. Peter then reminds them of their own frailty, again preaching the law to them: "All men are like grass. . . . the grass withers and the flowers fall." But God's Word, the Word that has given them new life, "stands forever." And so will they if they hold on to their faith.

Back and forth Peter goes, weaving a tapestry of sin and grace that will cover and shield his persecuted readers in all temptations.

We could go on and analyze 1 Peter 2:1-24 in the same way. But do this on your own. Isolate every verse in which the apostle instructs his readers to do something in service to God. Then ask yourself, What piece of gospel motivation is woven together with this admonition or encouragement? Then look carefully at the gospel encouragements. How many of the elements that we have looked at in the preceding chapters of this book can you find in these verses? Look for little words nestled in the text. Look at each word and phrase carefully. What thoughts does that word or phrase conjure up in your mind—about your relationship with God in Christ, how the Spirit is working in you through the various aspects of the gospel, or the hope you have in heaven?

As you meditate on these beautiful gospel phrases, see how they lift you up and create in you a desire to serve the Lord. Notice that when you come to the law passages—the passages that encourage sanctification—you find yourself willing and eager to follow them. They are no longer oppressive. They are no longer sources of guilt and frustration. They no longer stir up your sinful nature to rebel against the Lord. (Although as long as the sinful nature is present, it will try and use these passages against you.) Rather, these passages are welcome admonitions to serve the Lord, who redeemed you to himself.

Conclusion
Applications to the Ministry and Christian Service

This book has had one goal. It has looked at how Jesus and the New Testament writers encourage us to live lives in service to the Lord.

We have accomplished a few things toward that end. We have described the basic gospel on which the writers build their encouragement. We have also isolated various themes, all flowing directly out of the gospel, that the writers weave into their encouragement.

But there is much we have not done. We have not plumbed the depths of the complexity or the beauty of their writings. It is not something that can be sorted out and categorized as much as observed and admired. This is the Holy Spirit's way of speaking. The more you read the New Testament, the more you realize how perfect it is. Even if the New Testament did not say it was inspired by the Holy Spirit, you would come to that conclusion on your own by reading it.

Above all, we have seen the scriptural way of describing the relationship between our faith and our lives. We have explored the relationship between justification and sanctification, to use the dogmatics terms. And although there is a place for dogmatics books, no dogmatics book can really describe the relationship between these truths of our faith. Dogmatics books can describe what faith and life are. But only Scripture itself can guide us in how to best present these truths in a way that will build up God's people in the faith.

Studying the Bible on its own terms is vital for the Christian church. Bible studies on this or that doctrinal topic are fine. Studies to learn what the Bible says about this or that life issue are also fine. Studies about other denominations or world religions are helpful. But studies that pull this or that passage out of Scripture to draw a picture about the Bible's teaching on some topic can only take us so far. Invariably such studies miss what in many ways is the heart of Bible study, which is learning the depth of God's love in Christ and then living our lives as people who have come to know that love. Bible study in its purest form deals with our lives on the most basic level, our relationship with God and the life of service that must inevitably follow. It deals with God's love for us and our love for one another. It deals with sound teaching in its richest, most beautiful, and most edifying form.

At the beginning of this book, I said I hoped this study would help me in doing four things. I would like to return to those those four things.

The first goal of this study, for me at least, was to grow in my life of service. All I can say is what that teacher said in his old age: "I am not pious yet." I would like to think that somewhere down the road, there will be some halcyon days when everything will fall into place and a life of sanctification will be easy, or at least easier. I fear that is not to be.

Such an attitude does not flow from a *laissez-faire* attitude about sanctification, nor does it flow from defeatism. Rather, it flows from a realization that my sinful nature will always be there, keeping me from doing what I want. It also flows from a realization that God has his ways of increasing our faith and life and that giving in to the pressure of "being this" or "becoming that" because that's what a Christian should be like or that's the kind of victory God has promised his people is ill-fated and will lead us over to the dark side of piety.

Yet this study leads to great optimism. Christians are new beings. We have been re-created by the Lord, joined with Christ, and filled with the Holy Spirit. We know God's love, and through God's enlightenment we can and will grow to know God's love better, and that will lead us to greater service. We are works in progress.

We also have God's promise that he will grant us this growth. Paul reminds the Romans about God—"him who is able to establish you by my gospel and the proclamation of Jesus Christ, . . . the only wise God" (Romans 16:25-27).

We have Paul's prayers for us and God's promises that he relays to us. Paul prays:

> . . . that you, being rooted and established in love, may have power, together with all the saints, to grasp how wide and long and high and deep is the love of Christ, and to know this love that surpasses knowledge—that you may be filled to the measure of all the fullness of God. Now to him who is able to do immeasurably more than all we ask or imagine, according to his power that is at work within us, to him be glory in the church and in Christ Jesus throughout all generations, for ever and ever! (Ephesians 3:17-21)

Paul gives us his example and the Lord's encouragement:

> I press on toward the goal to win the prize for which God has called me heavenward in Christ Jesus. All of us who are mature should take such a view of things. And if on some point you think differently, that too God will make clear to you. Only let us live up to what we have already attained. (Philippians 3:14-16)

These promises give us great hope as we await the day when our Lord will take us to heaven:

> May God himself, the God of peace, sanctify you through and through. May your whole spirit, soul and body be kept blameless at the coming of our Lord Jesus Christ. The one who calls you is faithful and he will do it. (1 Thessalonians 5:23,24)

Such blamelessness begins with Christ, and it plays itself out in our lives so that when the Lord comes, he will find us, through the Spirit, putting to death the misdeeds of the body.

These promises lead us to strive, but they also allow us to handle our inadequacies, knowing the Lord is with us and will give us what we need to grow.

This study has shown us the pattern Christ and the apostles want us to follow as we help others in the faith. They want us to think continually about all that God has done for us. They want us to know God's unsurpassed love and grace and let that influence our thoughts and actions.

The second thing I was looking for is depth in applying the gospel to people's lives—or rather, placing people's lives into the context of the gospel, which is our source of hope and the reason we do what we do. We have made a good beginning at this. We could go much further. We have hardly captured the complete depth of the Holy Spirit's thought and expression.

Yet this study has given us a range of gospel truths that we can use when we encourage others in godly living. What's more, we have seen that the various situations we are called on to address are best dealt with when the right aspect of the gospel is applied to it. In other words, we have seen that Jesus and the apostles did not attach to every rebuke and encouragement the basic gospel message that Jesus loves us and has died for our sins.

Think of the breadth of the gospel as it is expressed in the sections of Scripture that urge holy living. Everything begins with Jesus' death on the cross for our sins and his resurrection. That is the heart of it all. Jesus' death and resurrection have made peace between God and the world. Through faith in this fact we become God's friends as he is already ours.

Romans 6 through 8 have set the foundation for all aspects of gospel motivation. These chapters described the spiritual sequence of events that began when we first believed and that have made us into people who are serving the Lord. We should speak more precisely, however. Our baptism, not our faith, enabled us to embark on the spiritual life we now enjoy. Of course, faith and Baptism are intertwined, but it was our baptism that joined us with Christ's death. And since Jesus rose from the dead, then we also rose from the dead and now live as people who have died and risen to serve our God, just as Jesus has.

Our death and resurrection in Christ gave us a new master, namely, the righteousness we have in Christ. We serve it; we shape our lives around it. We want nothing to do with our old master, sin, which leads to death. Our death and resurrection in Christ have also given us a new relation to the law. We are severed from it. It no longer says to us, "Do this, do that," stirring the sinful nature into action. We serve willingly, in a new and truly spiritual way, in freedom, motivated by the gospel and not by the law.

Although the sinful nature is always active and will be until we die, through God's Spirit—who has produced in us a "mind" that is focused on God and his will—we are not condemned. If, through the Spirit, we continue to put to death the misdeeds of the body, we will live.

We have become new creations. When God sees us, that's what he sees. As new people, made that way through our association with Christ's death and resurrection, we receive a whole array of blessings. We are part of a kingdom in which we are consoled by God's grace and by his power made secure in our faith. We have the hope of a heavenly kingdom in which God's presence and blessings will be ours for eternity. Living as members of God's kingdom is really living, for in this kingdom we experience all God's blessings and God does not withhold anything from us. Living as members of God's kingdom gives us hope, for our citizenship is in heaven; even now we have only one foot on earth. The other is planted where we will spend eternity. God speaks of rewards, which encourage us to hold on to our hope and not give up our labor for him.

God's kingdom is a kingdom of light, enlightened by Jesus, who is the Light of the world. We no longer walk in the darkness induced by ignorance of God's grace and by the law of sin and death. We walk in the light that began at our baptism and put us on the road to God built by Jesus' death and resurrection. These blessings are assured to us through the Lord's Supper, which gives us forgiveness in Christ and joins us with our brothers and sisters in Christ. Through the gospel we enjoy a fellowship that transcends blood relationships and makes us part of a group of people who share our hope. In that fellowship we have the support of fellow Christians whose prayers for our sanctification God will certainly answer.

This is the treasure we Christians have as we think about our own faith and life and when we encourage others. This is the treasure in our storeroom that we teachers have access to when we are given the call to teach others (Matthew 13:52). There is great variety here, and these truths can be tailored to fit any situation. As pastors follow the pattern of sound teaching exhibited in Scripture, they have every resource to give to their sermons the variety Jesus and Paul and the other apostles gave to theirs.

The third goal of this book was to explore the way Jesus and the apostles taught. Pastors have been taught the faith in an orderly, doctrinal way. It must be this way. It is too easy to express oneself incorrectly. History has shown the need to assemble passages that speak of the same truth and to present what they teach in an orderly way. This is merely letting Scripture interpret Scripture and learning to use Scripture to refute past and present errors and wrong ways of speaking. Without solid teaching in dogmatics, the church will wander this way and that.

That said, it is too easy for pastors in their sermons and church members in their conversations to express themselves in a rather formulaic way. This is not necessarily wrong. The problem is, however, that it often misses the beauty and fullness of how the apostles speak. It misses how the writers weave together justification and sanctification and, in a single sentence, can ground us in the former and encourage us in the latter.

It is good to read Jesus and the apostles not just to find passages that back up our Lutheran teaching but to seek to imitate their way of speaking. Thinking and speaking using only stock dogmatics formulas easily results in using only set modes of speech that employ little variety. Reading and studying Scripture with the intention of learning how the writers speak and how they teach sanctification will give us new and varied ways of speaking. It will help us weave these ways of speaking into our conversations, teaching, and counseling.

This is not to suggest that we become stilted and unnatural as we try to copy Scripture's way of speaking. Rather, we should talk as we normally talk, but we should incorporate all the aspects of the gospel into our speech and weave them in as we talk to others—letting our "conversation be always full of grace, seasoned with salt, so that you may know how to answer everyone" (Colossians 4:6).

We can weave the gospel into our conversations with our children, reminding them of their baptism and the new creatures they have become in Christ. We can weave the gospel into our conversations with fellow Christians when the conversation moves beyond the weather and gets into the problems and joys they are experiencing. We can weave the gospel in one of its many facets into our conversations with unbelieving friends at work when they ask us to give a reason for our hope.

Pastors who keep a list of gospel aspects before their eyes when they prepare sermons can more easily base their sermons on what congregation members already have in Christ. They can offer insight and direction from God's Word in a way that stresses the heart of why we serve the Lord. When gospel hope is before our eyes, moralizing becomes impossible.

Christian counselors especially can use the richness of the gospel in their work. Counseling can easily become merely giving practical advice on how to get along. Christian counseling is defined by how well the counselor leads people into the gospel, centering their lives not on their problems and complaints but on what they have been given and what they are in Christ.

The fourth reason for writing this book was to help us avoid the dark side of trying to live upright lives. What is the dark side of piety? It is the kind of piety that puts "me" at the center. My natural, sinful flesh wants to use piety to get something. That something could be God's favor. It could be personal happiness. It could be the results of a moral life on my health or relationships. It could even be eternal life.

The hardest of all the "me" motivations to diagnose and combat is the bare desire to become pious because that is what Christians are supposed to be. It is a yearning for piety because of the piety I see in others but that I have yet to achieve myself. It is the desire to be upright because that is the right way to be. It is the desire to find wholeness in my life, the kind that comes through not having to struggle against the sinful nature. The dark side of piety is recognized not only by a skewed desire for piety but also by what happens when we see what we consider to be progress or by what we are willing to do in order to achieve our goal. Pride, not joy, comes with growth in this kind of piety. The Christian's focus becomes his or her personal yearning, striving, obedience, and yielding. Christians may find themselves consumed with a desire for "something more," some infusion of virtue that will raise them up above the struggles that plague them and will give them the victory they so desperately want. A calm reliance and trust in the Lord and reliance on the power of his Word give way to impatience. Christians become open to human techniques and methods for growth and victory. They may even give in to other "spirits" that promise a "true conversion" into a state in which piety is easy. They may enjoy success for a time, but their spirit, since it is not from God's Spirit, will forsake them.

What a blessing it can be when children are urged to live upright lives throughout their youth. Those fortunate children with parents who urge them to serve the Lord and then give them the gospel in healthy doses—who remind them of God's forgiveness and are patient with them—will know how to grow in service to the Lord. Those, however, who are driven to piety without the gospel will invariably grow up with guilt and an internal desperation to serve the Lord and please their parents. Not knowing the gospel, they will fall into the dark side of piety.

Paradoxically, one of the greatest hindrances to true piety is this intense desire to become pious. The only antidote to this dark side is to learn about piety from Scripture and listen to the inspired writers encourage us to Christian living in a way that revolves around the gospel.

Paul knew there were methods people chose to foster moral lives that were both useless and against the apostles' teaching:

> Since you died with Christ to the basic principles of this world, why, as though you still belonged to it, do you submit to its rules: "Do not handle! Do not taste! Do not touch!"? These are all destined to perish with use, because they are based on human commands and teachings. Such regulations indeed have an appearance of wisdom, with their self-imposed worship, their false humility and their harsh treatment of the body, but they lack any value in restraining sensual indulgence. (Colossians 2:20-23)

Some people, Paul says, rely on rules to manufacture godliness. They seem to be living their lives wisely. They worship God; they are humble; in fact, they treat their bodies harshly, similar to how Paul beat his body to bring it into submission (1 Corinthians 9:27). Yet since their piety is self-generated and their methods are self-chosen, they can do nothing to create in themselves the power to restrain sensual indulgence.

Scripture alone gives us the way God wants us to grow in faith. The gospel is to be the center of our lives. We grow in piety because we have a hope centered in Christ. We grow in holy living the more we realize how wonderful God's love is. We grow in our ability to serve the more the new man is built up through the knowledge of its freedom from the law. We die to our old life the more we realize what a privilege it is to have died and risen with Jesus by faith.

We cannot program this growth. We can only trust that God will give it to us, as the Bible promises. We cannot demand this or that degree of growth. We can only go to the Scriptures and the Lord's Supper and remember our baptism and there find the assurance of our hope. God will give us the Holy Spirit as he leads us to understand the depth of God's grace.

It is tempting to look beyond this for more. But Scripture gives us no more, and the apostles, as they pray for us in their writings, include no more. Our goal is to live up to what we already have and pray confidently for more, not to satisfy our own desires for piety but to please the Lord who has called us into his kingdom. As you seek to grow, never assume that you know the gospel already and now only need to hear what you should do. Rather, approach it in the opposite direction. Realize that you (if you have been a Christian for long) already know what to do, and now you only need to grow in knowing the gospel better. Growth in true spiritual wisdom and knowledge, centered on the gospel, will enable you to advance on the path of Christian living.

May the Lord grant such growth to all his people.

Study Questions

Chapter 1: The Gospel of God's Love and Forgiveness in Christ

Chapter 2: The Gospel of Death and Life

1. The gospel is never a means to an end but the end itself. Why must this be the starting point for talking about gospel motivation?

2. Spreading the gospel, nurturing the faith and lives of God's people—this is God's agenda. Why is it so important that we line up our agendas with God's agenda? Why does this keep us from "using" the gospel in the wrong way?

3. Why does "using" the gospel tend to downplay the greatness of the gospel?

4. What does the author mean by the "gospel of death"?

5. What is the "gospel of life"?

6. How did you die and rise again?

7. Practice finding gospel motivation in the following passages. Put parentheses around the gospel, and underline what the Bible writer encourages us to do because of the gospel. (Passages are taken from chapter 1.)

At one time we too were foolish, disobedient, deceived and enslaved by all kinds of passions and pleasures. We lived in malice and envy, being hated and hating one another. But when the kindness and love of God our Savior appeared, he saved us, not because of righteous things we had done, but because of his mercy. He saved us through the washing of rebirth and renewal by the Holy Spirit, whom he poured out on us generously through Jesus Christ our Savior, so that, having been justified by his grace, we might become heirs having the hope of eternal life. This is a trustworthy saying. And I want you to stress these things, so that those who have trusted in God may be careful to devote themselves to doing what is good. These things are excellent and profitable for everyone. (Titus 3:3-8)

How great is the love the Father has lavished on us, that we should be called children of God! And that is what we are! The reason the world does not know us is that it did not know him. Dear friends, now we are children of God, and what we will be has not yet been made known. But we know that when he appears, we shall be like him, for we shall see him as he is. Everyone who has this hope in him purifies himself, just as he is pure. (1 John 3:1-3)

This is how God showed his love among us: He sent his one and only Son into the world that we might live through him. This is love: not that we loved God, but that he loved us and sent his Son as an atoning sacrifice for our sins. Dear friends, since God so loved us, we also ought to love one another. We love because he first loved us. (1 John 4:9-11,19)

As a prisoner for the Lord, then, I urge you to live a life worthy of the calling you have received. (Ephesians 4:1)

Bear with each other and forgive whatever grievances you may have against one another. Forgive as the Lord forgave you. (Colossians 3:13)

Be kind and compassionate to one another, forgiving each other, just as in Christ God forgave you. Be imitators of God, therefore, as dearly loved children and live a life of love, just as Christ loved us and gave himself up for us as a fragrant offering and sacrifice to God. (Ephesians 4:32–5:2)

For this very reason, make every effort to add to your faith goodness; and to goodness, knowledge; and to knowledge, self-control; and to self-control, perseverance; and to perseverance, godliness; and to godliness, brotherly kindness; and to brotherly kindness, love. For if you possess these qualities in increasing measure, they will keep you from being ineffective and unproductive in your knowledge of our Lord Jesus Christ. But if anyone does not have them, he is nearsighted and blind, and has forgotten that he has been cleansed from his past sins. (2 Peter 1:5-9)

Your boasting is not good. Don't you know that a little yeast works through the whole batch of dough? Get rid of the old yeast that you may be a new batch without yeast—as you really are. For Christ, our Passover lamb, has been sacrificed. Therefore let us keep the Festival, not with the old yeast, the yeast of malice and wickedness, but with bread without yeast, the bread of sincerity and truth. (1 Corinthians 5:6-8)

The grace of God that brings salvation has appeared to all men. It teaches us to say "No" to ungodliness and worldly passions, and to live self-controlled, upright and godly lives in this present age, while we wait for the blessed hope—the glorious appearing of our great God and Savior, Jesus Christ, who gave himself for us to redeem us from all wickedness and to purify for himself a people that are his very own, eager to do what is good. These, then, are the things you should teach. Encourage and rebuke with all authority. Do not let anyone despise you. (Titus 2:11-15)

Chapter 3: The Gospel of Slavery to Righteousness

Chapter 4: The Gospel of True Spirituality

1. What are the two options in a Christian's life? Why can there never be a state of neutrality in regard to these two options?

2. Romans 6:16 is an important verse. What does Paul mean by the "obedience, which leads to righteousness"? Why is it important to understand this phrase properly?

3. How do people who have received Christ's righteousness think of their relationship to sin? to a righteous life?

4. Describe the joy of being a slave to God.

5. Explain the relationship between head and heart in relation to our faith. Note Ephesians 3:16-19.

6. What is the best way for a teacher to speak to both the head and the heart of a Christian?

7. Describe how some people in our world define the word *spiritual*.

8. What is God's definition of true spirituality?

9. How are we able to live in the new way of the Spirit?

10. Did the two pictures presented in chapter 4 help you capture a sense of freedom that led to a willingness to serve?

11. Why does the law do the opposite of making us willing to keep it?

12. If we serve in the new way of the Spirit, why do we still sin?

13. Define spiritual growth in terms of the new creation and the old sinful flesh.

14. Practice finding gospel motivation in the following passages. Put parentheses around the gospel, and underline what the Bible writer encourages us to do because of the gospel. (Passages are taken from chapter 2.)

> What shall we say, then? Shall we go on sinning so that grace may increase? By no means! We died to sin; how can we live in it any longer? (Romans 6:1,2)

> Do not let sin reign in your mortal body so that you obey its evil desires. Do not offer the parts of your body to sin, as instruments of wickedness, but rather offer yourselves to God, as those who have been brought from death to life; and offer the parts of your body to him as instruments of righteousness. (Romans 6:12,13)

> Through the law I died to the law so that I might live for God. I have been crucified with Christ and I no longer live, but Christ lives in me. The life I live in the body, I live by faith in the Son of God, who loved me and gave himself for me. (Galatians 2:19,20)

> Since you died with Christ to the basic principles of this world, why, as though you still belonged to it, do you submit to its rules: "Do not handle! Do not taste! Do not touch!"? (Colossians 2:20,21)

> Since, then, you have been raised with Christ, set your hearts on things above, where Christ is seated at the right hand of God. Set your minds on things above, not on earthly things. For you died, and your life is now hidden with Christ in God. When Christ, who is your life, appears, then you also will appear with him in glory. Put to death, therefore, whatever belongs to your earthly nature: sexual immorality, impurity, lust, evil desires and greed, which is idolatry. (Colossians 3:1-5)

> Christ's love compels us, because we are convinced that one died for all, and therefore all died. And he died for all, that those who live should no longer live for themselves but for him who died for them and was raised again. (2 Corinthians 5:14,15)

Chapter 5: The Gospel of a New Creation

Chapter 6: The Gospel of How God Views New Creations

1. Describe how we became new creations.

2. According to Paul in Romans 8, why are we not condemned?

3. How did God enable us to become new creations?

4. In Romans 8:12 Paul speaks of an obligation. What is our obligation, and why do we have it?

5. Some passages in Scripture link the works of our new man to the blessings we receive from God. Why do you think these passages have been misunderstood? What false teachings have such passages been used to support? In your own words, explain these passages in the way Scripture intends them to be understood.

6. List some of the blessings that are given to those who serve the Lord.

7. Practice finding gospel motivation in the following passages. Put parentheses around the gospel, and underline what the Bible writer encourages us to do because of the gospel. (Passages are taken from chapters 5 and 6.)

> He died for all, that those who live should no longer live for themselves but for him who died for them and was raised again. So from now on we regard no one from a worldly point of view. Though we once regarded Christ in this way, we do so no longer. Therefore, if anyone is in Christ, he is a new creation; the old has gone, the new has come! (2 Corinthians 5:15-17)

> Do not lie to each other, since you have taken off your old self with its practices and have put on the new self, which is being renewed in knowledge in the image of its Creator. (Colossians 3:9,10)

Love your enemies, do good to them, and lend to them without expecting to get anything back. Then your reward will be great, and you will be sons of the Most High, because he is kind to the ungrateful and wicked. Be merciful, just as your Father is merciful. (Luke 6:35,36)

I am the true vine, and my Father is the gardener. He cuts off every branch in me that bears no fruit, while every branch that does bear fruit he prunes so that it will be even more fruitful. You are already clean because of the word I have spoken to you. Remain in me, and I will remain in you. No branch can bear fruit by itself; it must remain in the vine. Neither can you bear fruit unless you remain in me. I am the vine; you are the branches. If a man remains in me and I in him, he will bear much fruit; apart from me you can do nothing. This is to my Father's glory, that you bear much fruit, showing yourselves to be my disciples. (John 15:1-5,8)

Dear children, let us not love with words or tongue but with actions and in truth. This then is how we know that we belong to the truth, and how we set our hearts at rest in his presence whenever our hearts condemn us. For God is greater than our hearts, and he knows everything. Dear friends, if our hearts do not condemn us, we have confidence before God and receive from him anything we ask, because we obey his commands and do what pleases him. And this is his command: to believe in the name of his Son, Jesus Christ, and to love one another as he commanded us. Those who obey his commands live in him, and he in them. (1 John 3:18-24)

God is love. Whoever lives in love lives in God, and God in him. In this way, love is made complete among us so that we will have confidence on the day of judgment, because in this world we are like him. There is no fear in love. But perfect love drives out fear, because fear has to do with punishment. The one who fears is not made perfect in love. We love because he first loved us. If anyone says, "I love God," yet hates his brother, he is a liar. For anyone who does not love his brother, whom he has seen, cannot love God, whom he has not seen. (1 John 4:16-20)

The man who loves his life will lose it, while the man who hates his life in this world will keep it for eternal life. Whoever serves me must follow me; and where I am, my servant also will be. My Father will honor the one who serves me. (John 12:25,26)

God "will give to each person according to what he has done." To those who by persistence in doing good seek glory, honor and immortality, he will give eternal life. But for those who are self-seeking and who reject the truth and follow evil, there will be wrath and anger. There will be trouble and distress for every human being who does evil: first for the Jew, then for the Gentile; but glory, honor and peace for everyone who does good: first for the Jew, then for the Gentile. For God does not show favoritism. (Romans 2:6-11)

Do not be deceived: God cannot be mocked. A man reaps what he sows. The one who sows to please his sinful nature, from that nature will reap destruction; the one who sows to please the Spirit, from the Spirit will reap eternal life. Let us not become weary in doing good, for at the proper time we will reap a harvest if we do not give up. (Galatians 6:7-9)

Just as he who called you is holy, so be holy in all you do; for it is written: "Be holy, because I am holy." Since you call on a Father who judges each man's work impartially, live your lives as strangers here in reverent fear. For you know that it was not with perishable things such as silver or gold that you were redeemed from the empty way of life handed down to you from your forefathers, but with the precious blood of Christ, a lamb without blemish or defect. He was chosen before the creation of the world, but was revealed in these last times for your sake. (1 Peter 1:15-20)

Everyone who has left houses or brothers or sisters or father or mother or children or fields for my sake will receive a hundred times as much and will inherit eternal life. (Matthew 19:29)

Then the King will say to those on his right, "Come, you who are blessed by my Father; take your inheritance, the kingdom prepared for you since the creation of the world. For I was hungry and you gave me something to eat, I was thirsty and you gave me something to drink, I was a stranger and you invited me in." (Matthew 25:34,35)

My dear brothers, stand firm. Let nothing move you. Always give yourselves fully to the work of the Lord, because you know that your labor in the Lord is not in vain. (1 Corinthians 15:58)

Chapter 7: The Gospel of the Kingdom

Chapter 8: The Gospel in the Sacraments; The Gospel of Light

1. Where did the concept of the kingdom of God begin?

2. What sort of kingdom was Israel looking forward to?

3. What role did the following play in God's kingdom?

   • miracles

   • parables

   • Jesus' death and resurrection

4. What does it mean for you that you are now living in Christ's kingdom?

5. Where is gospel motivation found in the Sermon on the Mount?

6. What does it mean for you to live in God's kingdom?

7. What does it mean to remember your baptism?

8. How did Paul solve the problem of favoritism in Corinth?

9. Practice finding gospel motivation in the following passages. Put parentheses around the gospel, and underline what the Bible writer encourages us to do because of the gospel. (Passages are taken from chapters 7 and 8.)

   We pray this in order that you may live a life worthy of the Lord and may please him in every way: bearing fruit in every good work, growing in the knowledge of God, being strengthened with all power according to his glorious might so that you may have great endurance and patience, and joyfully giving thanks to the Father, who has qualified you to share in the inheritance of the saints in the kingdom of light. For he has rescued us from the dominion of darkness and brought us into the kingdom of the Son he loves, in whom we have redemption, the forgiveness of sins. (Colossians 1:10-14)

You are a chosen people, a royal priesthood, a holy nation, a people belonging to God, that you may declare the praises of him who called you out of darkness into his wonderful light. Once you were not a people, but now you are the people of God; once you had not received mercy, but now you have received mercy. Dear friends, I urge you, as aliens and strangers in the world, to abstain from sinful desires, which war against your soul. (1 Peter 2:9-11)

See to it that no one takes you captive through hollow and deceptive philosophy, which depends on human tradition and the basic principles of this world rather than on Christ. For in Christ all the fullness of the Deity lives in bodily form, and you have been given fullness in Christ, who is the head over every power and authority. In him you were also circumcised, in the putting off of the sinful nature, not with a circumcision done by the hands of men but with the circumcision done by Christ, having been buried with him in baptism and raised with him through your faith in the power of God, who raised him from the dead. When you were dead in your sins and in the uncircumcision of your sinful nature, God made you alive with Christ. He forgave us all our sins, having canceled the written code, with its regulations, that was against us and that stood opposed to us; he took it away, nailing it to the cross. (Colossians 2:8-14)

Remind the people to be subject to rulers and authorities, to be obedient, to be ready to do whatever is good, to slander no one, to be peaceable and considerate, and to show true humility toward all men. . . . But when the kindness and love of God our Savior appeared, he saved us, not because of righteous things we had done, but because of his mercy. He saved us through the washing of rebirth and renewal by the Holy Spirit, whom he poured out on us generously through Jesus Christ our Savior, so that, having been justified by his grace, we might become heirs having the hope of eternal life. This is a trustworthy saying. And I want you to stress these things, so that those who have trusted in God may be careful to devote themselves to doing what is good. (Titus 3:1-8)

The night is nearly over; the day is almost here. So let us put aside the deeds of darkness and put on the armor of light. Let us behave decently, as in the daytime, not in orgies and drunkenness, not in sexual immorality and debauchery, not in dissension and jealousy. Rather, clothe yourselves with the Lord Jesus Christ, and do not think about how to gratify the desires of the sinful nature. (Romans 13:12-14)

You are all sons of the light and sons of the day. We do not belong to the night or to the darkness. So then, let us not be like others, who are asleep, but let us be alert and self-controlled. For those who sleep, sleep at night, and those who get drunk, get drunk at night. But since we belong to the day, let us be self-controlled, putting on faith and love as a breastplate, and the hope of salvation as a helmet. For God did not appoint us to suffer wrath but to receive salvation through our Lord Jesus Christ. (1 Thessalonians 5:5-9)

Chapter 9: The Gospel of Eternal Life

Chapter 10: The Gospel of Our Fellowship in Christ; Prayers for One Another

1. What is the end of our faith?

2. Why is our fellowship with other Christians an aspect of the gospel message?

3. How does our bond of faith with fellow Christians motivate us to serve them and God?

4. How many times does Paul use the words "in Christ" or "in faith" in Romans 16:1-16?

5. How does his use of these terms shape his attitude toward his fellow believers?

6. Why is prayer so important for our lives of faith and our growth in faith?

7. Pick one of the prayer verses in this chapter and tell what we should pray for on behalf of our fellow Christians.

8. Practice finding gospel motivation in the following passages. Put parentheses around the gospel, and underline what the Bible writer encourages us to do because of the gospel. (Passages are taken from chapters 9 and 10.)

> Do this, understanding the present time. The hour has come for you to wake up from your slumber, because our salvation is nearer now than when we first believed. The night is nearly over; the day is almost here. So let us put aside the deeds of darkness and put on the armor of light. Let us behave decently, as in the daytime, not in orgies and drunkenness, not in sexual immorality and debauchery, not in dissension and jealousy. Rather, clothe yourselves with the Lord Jesus Christ, and do not think about how to gratify the desires of the sinful nature. (Romans 13:11-14)

> But you, man of God, flee from all this, and pursue righteousness, godliness, faith, love, endurance and gentleness. Fight the good fight of the faith. Take hold of the eternal life to which you were called when you made your good confession in the presence of many witnesses. In the sight of God, who gives life to everything, and of Christ Jesus, who while testifying before Pontius Pilate made the good confession, I charge you to keep this command without spot or blame until the appearing of our Lord Jesus Christ, which God will bring about in his own time—God, the blessed and only Ruler, the King of kings and Lord of lords. (1 Timothy 6:11-15)

> The grace of God that brings salvation has appeared to all men. It teaches us to say "No" to ungodliness and worldly passions, and to live self-controlled, upright

and godly lives in this present age, while we wait for the blessed hope—the glorious appearing of our great God and Savior, Jesus Christ, who gave himself for us to redeem us from all wickedness and to purify for himself a people that are his very own, eager to do what is good. (Titus 2:11-14)

Let us not give up meeting together, as some are in the habit of doing, but let us encourage one another— and all the more as you see the Day approaching. If we deliberately keep on sinning after we have received the knowledge of the truth, no sacrifice for sins is left, but only a fearful expectation of judgment and of raging fire that will consume the enemies of God. (Hebrews 10:25-27)

Prepare your minds for action; be self-controlled; set your hope fully on the grace to be given you when Jesus Christ is revealed. As obedient children, do not conform to the evil desires you had when you lived in ignorance. (1 Peter 1:13,14)

The day of the Lord will come like a thief. The heavens will disappear with a roar; the elements will be destroyed by fire, and the earth and everything in it will be laid bare. Since everything will be destroyed in this way, what kind of people ought you to be? You ought to live holy and godly lives as you look forward to the day of God and speed its coming. That day will bring about the destruction of the heavens by fire, and the elements will melt in the heat. But in keeping with his promise we are looking forward to a new heaven and a new earth, the home of righteousness. So then, dear friends, since you are looking forward to this, make every effort to be found spotless, blameless and at peace with him. (2 Peter 3:10-14)

If your brother is distressed because of what you eat, you are no longer acting in love. Do not by your eating destroy your brother for whom Christ died. Do not destroy the work of God for the sake of food. All food is clean, but it is wrong for a man to eat anything that causes someone else to stumble. (Romans 14:15,20)

Be completely humble and gentle; be patient, bearing with one another in love. Make every effort to keep the unity of the Spirit through the bond of peace. There is one body and one Spirit—just as you were called to one hope when you were called—one Lord, one faith, one baptism; one God and Father of all, who is over all and through all and in all. Therefore each of you must put off falsehood and speak truthfully to his neighbor, for we are all members of one body. (Ephesians 4:2-6,25)

Chapter 11: Special Examples, Part 1

Chapter 12: Special Examples, Part 2

1. Describe how Paul motivates husbands and wives in their respective roles (Ephesians 5).

2. What is the most practical thing Scripture teaches us? How does this shape a congregation's order of priorities? a pastor's ministry?

3. Why should a church focus on "God's things" and not just "good things"? What's the difference between the two?

4. The author writes, "Only what transcends this life is truly practical." Do you think he is right?

5. How does Paul lead the Corinthians to view the following problems?

   Chapter 5, the matter of incest

   Chapter 6:1-11, lawsuits

   Chapter 6:12-20, sexual immorality

   Chapter 8, food sacrificed to idols

   Chapter 10, idol feasts

   Chapter 11, separatism and favoritism in worship services

6. Think about Colossians 3:1-4. What profound view do you have of yourself as you read these verses?

7. How does Paul encourage stewardship in 2 Corinthians 8 and 9?

8. Read and analyze 1 Peter 2:1-24.

9. Practice finding gospel motivation in the following passages. Put parentheses around the gospel, and underline what the Bible writer encourages us to do because of the gospel. (Passages are taken from chapter 12.)

> Since, then, you have been raised with Christ, set your hearts on things above, where Christ is seated at the right hand of God. Set your minds on things above, not on earthly things. For you died, and your life is now hidden with Christ in God. When Christ, who is your life, appears, then you also will appear with him in glory. (Colossians 3:1-4)

> Put to death, therefore, whatever belongs to your earthly nature: sexual immorality, impurity, lust, evil desires and greed, which is idolatry. Because of these, the wrath of God is coming. You used to walk in these ways, in the life you once lived. But now you must rid yourselves of all such things as these: anger, rage, malice, slander, and filthy language from your lips. Do not lie to each other, since you have taken off your old self with its practices and have put on the new self, which is being renewed in knowledge in the image of its Creator. (Colossians 3:5-10)

> Here there is no Greek or Jew, circumcised or uncircumcised, barbarian, Scythian, slave or free, but Christ is all, and is in all. Therefore, as God's chosen people, holy and dearly loved, clothe yourselves with compassion, kindness, humility, gentleness and patience. Bear with each other and forgive whatever grievances you may have against one another. Forgive as the Lord forgave you. And over all these virtues put on love, which binds them all together in perfect unity. Let the peace of Christ rule in your hearts, since as members of one body you were called to peace. And be

thankful. Let the word of Christ dwell in you richly as you teach and admonish one another with all wisdom, and as you sing psalms, hymns and spiritual songs with gratitude in your hearts to God. And whatever you do, whether in word or deed, do it all in the name of the Lord Jesus, giving thanks to God the Father through him. (Colossians 3:11-17)

Do not let any unwholesome talk come out of your mouths, but only what is helpful for building others up according to their needs, that it may benefit those who listen. And do not grieve the Holy Spirit of God, with whom you were sealed for the day of redemption. Get rid of all bitterness, rage and anger, brawling and slander, along with every form of malice. Be kind and compassionate to one another, forgiving each other, just as in Christ God forgave you.

Be imitators of God, therefore, as dearly loved children and live a life of love, just as Christ loved us and gave himself up for us as a fragrant offering and sacrifice to God. But among you there must not be even a hint of sexual immorality, or of any kind of impurity, or of greed, because these are improper for God's holy people. Nor should there be obscenity, foolish talk or coarse joking, which are out of place, but rather thanksgiving. For of this you can be sure: No immoral, impure or greedy person—such a man is an idolater—has any inheritance in the kingdom of Christ and of God.

Let no one deceive you with empty words, for because of such things God's wrath comes on those who are disobedient. Therefore do not be partners with them. For you were once darkness, but now you are light in the Lord. Live as children of light (for the fruit of the light consists in all goodness, righteousness and truth) and find out what pleases the Lord. (Ephesians 4:29–5:10)

Scripture Index

11:25—70
12:30—41

Luke

1:69-75—93
1:71—94
2:30-32—112
6:35,36—71,177
7:40-47—71
7:50—71
10:20—95
12:38—83
17:10—38
21:28—153

John

1:4-9—112
3:18-20—74
3:19-21—112,113
8:12—113
12:25,26—83,177,178
12:31,32—31
12:35,36—113
12:46—113
13:34,35—72
14:22-24—72
15—72,73
15:1-5,8—73,177
15:5—26,28,46
15:9-14—73

Acts

9:1-6—15
15:16,17—97
28:30,31—101

Romans

1–5—24
1:1—38
1:17—35,36

2:6-11—83,178
3–5—8,61
3:21-5—56
3:24,28—61
4—79
4:4-8—61
4:16—79
6—24-28,32-42,60,136,
   140
6,7—24,107,152
6–8—56,58,64,72,81,
   82,164
6:1,2—24,175
6:1-13—23-27
6:1–8:17—105
6:3—40
6:3,4—25
6:5—25
6:6—40
6:6-8—26
6:8—40
6:9—40
6:9-11—26
6:11—25,40
6:12—37
6:12,13—27,175
6:13—144
6:14—27,34
6:14-23—33-39
6:15—36
6:16—34,35,36,40,174
6:16-18—35
6:17—35,40
6:18—35
6:19—38
6:19-22—37
6:22—36
6:23—37,60
7—24,50,51,58
7,8—63
7:1-3—45
7:1-6—24,38,43-45,52

1 Corinthians

2 Corinthians